THE IMMORTAL KING

THE IMMORTAL KING

Yama

Sudhamahi Regunathan

BLOOMSBURY
NEW DELHI • LONDON • OXFORD • NEW YORK • SYDNEY

BLOOMSBURY INDIA
Bloomsbury Publishing India Pvt. Ltd
Second Floor, LSC Building No. 4, DDA Complex, Pocket C – 6 & 7,
Vasant Kunj, New Delhi, 110070

BLOOMSBURY, BLOOMSBURY INDIA and the Diana logo
are trademarks of Bloomsbury Publishing Plc

First published in India 2026

ISBN: PB: 978-93-61310-38-6; eBook: 978-93-61312-54-0

2 4 6 8 10 9 7 5 3 1

Typeset in Fournier MT Manipal Technologies Limited
Printed and bound in India by Thomson Press India Private Limited

MIX
Paper | Supporting responsible forestry
FSC® C010615
FSC www.fsc.org

To find out more about our authors and books visit www.bloomsbury.com
and sign up for our newsletters

To Yama

Great company off duty

CONTENTS

Introduction

Conversations have their own flavour. Words exchanged form only a part of it. Our biases and prejudices, our mood, the ambience, the hierarchy and the unspoken add up to give meaning to the conversation. Therefore, when the most feared king, who has not been classified as a god despite being truly omniscient, converses, the conversation becomes catalytic and compelling.

This king is the king of Death, Yama. The idea itself is dumbfounding. Death, as we know it, does not indulge in conversation. Maybe a little negotiation as we run between hospitals and medicines, but beyond that there is no repeal. That is the drama about him. He does not relent.

Or does he?

Discovering the heart of Yama was the endeavour of this book. When Yami, his twin sister, proposes intimacy with him, Yama's discomfiture and refined manner of dealing with it gave me my first glimpse of it.

His name Yama was associated with the meaning of *yamaka* or *yamaja*, which means twin in Sanskrit. Later his name was believed to be derived from the Sanskrit root word *yam*, which means to control. It could also be related to *yantrana*, meaning pain, distress, suffering. So Yama became the one who caused such pain. Just as one word could find many meanings, the king of death too found that people perceived him in many ways. Yama changed in the popular perception and conception in the texts from a benevolent guide to an evil, dark force (with a green face and two horns to boot). In the Vedas he is identified more as the one who shows the path to the place where souls rest before being born again. He is a handsome man, akin to Vishnu. The place to which he found the path was called Samyamanapuri – a very beautiful place, we are told. Samyamanapuri lay even beyond the sun.

Yama's association with the sun through time, the sun being the measure of our years and life, is mythologically described as Yama being the son of sun. By the time of the Upanishads, Indian thought had found many new dimensions opening up, some as challenges and some as reinforcements of its beliefs. The growth of Jainism and Buddhism placed great emphasis on karma and rebirth. Liberation and reincarnation became two ends of the scale of possibilities. Once liberated, the soul is not reborn in the mortal world. The doctrine of the migration of souls after death from one being to another, metempsychosis, came into prominence. Therefore, a complex matrix of reward and punishment was born.

Hades, the god of death, and Persephone from Greek mythology, the Roman Pluto and texts like the Avesta, to mention some, in many direct and indirect ways, have also influenced the profile of Yama as the local changes were taking place. Personal deities gained prominence and Yama was absorbed into the larger idea of Siva.

Did Yama actually change? Did he become a judge from a guide? Did he become cruel from being gentle?

In 1999, when I was interviewing Katun Borang (who was then director, Arts and Culture, Government of Arunachal Pradesh), I asked him, 'What happens after death?' I was trying to understand the faith of Donyipoloism that five tribes of Arunachal Pradesh followed. Borang was a follower of the faith. The question was asked in that context. Borang replied, 'I do not know. I have not yet died.'[1]

That remains for me the most profound statement yet.

My excursions to understand and explore Yama's conversations should be looked at in this light. Mythology and practice may have changed with times. Today we are beneficiaries of all those ideas born in different time periods and circumstances. Drawing upon all of them, I have tried to understand Yama. I have referred to different texts, translations, commentaries and explanations and have adhered to the original Sanskrit verses. The interpretations, however, are my own, influenced by wanting to tell a story.

The story of a unique kind of woman, Savitri, who was able to face Yama. My throat becomes parched, my insides wobble and I lose my voice at the mere thought of Yama coming anywhere around me. How did Savitri talk to him? The extraordinariness of such a courageous personality is often dimmed by the emphasis on her being a 'pativrata' or devoted to her husband. When my grandmother told me this story, she always had a footnote, 'That is how every woman should be.' But Savitri was painting a much larger picture. To be devoted to the husband, a lovely idea though it is, is not the end of it. She did not whine, whimper or turn helpless when Yama came. She faced him with composure. Her own scholarship, penance and adherence to her duty as a householder came together in the form a strong woman who could save her love even in the face of death. Savitri says in her conversation with Yama that one does not have to wait for the stage of vanaprastha[2] to seek Brahman. If you perform your duty, completely and honestly, whatever stage of life you are in, be you a wife or a husband, a son or a student, you are adhering to dharma. Her manner of conversation is sophisticated and strategic.

I have always felt a little disappointed to hear that the teaching that Yama gave to Nachiketas was the short cut to Brahman, which is Om. Disappointed, because it does not leave me any wiser and would require many years of practice to understand, and perhaps never to realise. Though not completely a part of the instant-gratification generation, I still wanted something more tangible and that I got when Yama told Nachiketas, 'The self is the highest, there is nothing greater. In you lies Brahman, *etadvai tat* [this is that], and there is nothing greater than you.' What a strong revelation! Indeed, the mahavakyas[3] of the Hindu religion have said this again and again, but it still carries force and novelty each time it is said, more so coming as it does after a discussion between a little boy called Nachiketas and Yama himself.

The conversation with Yudhishthira is enough material for a separate book. However, the attempt has been to weave the stories that support/illustrate the answer of Yudhishthira while still being associated with Yama. Yama is only thought of as the one who brings death. But he has also faced many interesting situations including being an aspiring suitor for Damayanti.[4] The different mythological stories may not be chronologically well matched. Time is not of relevance since both, the question and the story, are being delivered to us at the same time. To illustrate one with the other brings the cogency and completeness of the mythology sharply and dexterously into focus.

Does all communication have to be verbal? Yama has not stopped communication. As late as in the nineteenth century, he spoke with Ramana Maharishi, albeit in silence. He, Yama, lets the great sage experience him and discover who he is. Time and order (kala and rhta) are the two coordinates in the life of Yama. To illustrate Ramana's experiences, therefore, philosophers from the contemporary world have been quoted.

Thus it is that the road to immortality is constructed. To the uninclined too I feel the idea of Yama has some beauty, for beauty by itself and the beauty of love is the immortal we are seeking.

Book 1

THE HANDSOME SON

I

The making of Yama

He was the complexion of a rain cloud. Tall and well built, he was very handsome. He put on garments of burnt gold and chose his jewellery with care. Suddenly he became aware that he was not alone. Watching him was Yami. It was the look in her eyes that disturbed him. He turned away quickly. But she had caught his eye and now called out to him, saying:

> In this desolate and expansive place,
> Alone with you, my very dear friend,
> I yearn to become one with you, my twin,
> Bear with me a child who will do you and our father proud.[1]

Yama was shocked. How could his twin sister talk to him so!

They were the children of Surya, also known as Vivaswan. Their mother, Sanjna,[2] was daughter of Tvasthr, the skilful craftsman who had created many iconic implements, including Indra's bolt and Brihaspati's axe. Sanjna was also called Saranyu, which meant 'one who is swift'. Indeed, she was well matched to the effulgent sun.

As newlyweds, Surya and Sanjna had been happy. They loved one another dearly. But there was one problem. Surya was very radiant. His brilliance was so blinding that every time Surya turned to look at his bride with love and tenderness, she would shut her eyes. Unable to bear the glare of Surya's brilliance, Sanjna's eyes closed reflexively whenever his eyes fell upon her. Sanjna was enamoured of her husband, but his brilliance was a bit too much. She could not keep her eyes open to meet his. When this happened again and again, Surya got a little upset. 'Why would you do that? I feel you do not want to see me,' he said to his wife. But the very next time he turned to look at her, she shut her eyes yet again.

> When Ravi (Surya) turned to look at his bride
>   Sanjna, she shut her eyes in reflex
> And then annoyed, he said to her with irritation:

'Every time I try to catch your eye, you restrain that
contact by closing them,
So a son you will give birth to, you silly one, who is
a restrainer of all living beings.'[3]

Sanjna was shocked. Surya had got angry with her! And had cursed her child in the womb! Worried, she quickly opened her eyes and tried to face Surya. Her head hurt, her eyes closed involuntarily, but she bravely tried to keep them open. However, she had to narrow her eyes to do so, and as she struggled with the effort of it, she ended up blinking. Seeing the terror and agitation in her eyes, the eyeballs darting hither and thither like a frightened deer's, Surya went on to tell her that she would bear a daughter too, as fickle as her eyesight, who would flow as a river.

Thereupon the goddess, unnerved by fear, became
wild-eyed,
And Sun, seeing her agitated glances, addressed her
again,
'Since your eyes have become agitated and your
vision fickle on seeing me,
You shall give birth to a daughter who is restless.
She will be a river.'

Yama was born,[4] with his future thus predestined. And as prophesied, Yami was born too, as his twin sister. Later she would turn into the river Yamuna. It was this sister of Yama's who was proposing intimacy with him now.

Yama replied to her, even while his eyes scanned the landscape to see if anyone was within hearing distance:

> Your friend Yama does not desire such a relationship
> with you, who are no stranger to me
> Being a sibling, you are not the right one to mate with
> Remember, the powerful creator and his many eyes
> Are watching us all the time.

Yami frowned. Her sister Soorya[5] had recently got married to Soma, the moon. A vivid picture of their wedding formed before her eyes. Soorya had been all dressed up, her eyes lined with kohl. She was escorted to her husband, who had lovingly told their father to send her at an auspicious moment to him so that she would 'wrap her arms around me in love, and receive with joy, all my love and my embraces'.[6]

Yami shook herself out of her reverie and laughed scornfully. She was now full of lust. She wanted Yama. Am I suggesting something that is unheard of or what the gods have not indulged in? she wondered indignantly.

> Gods have had such relationships, it is forbidden
> only for mortals

> Turn your mind towards me, and like the gods bear
> your offspring.

Yama replied rather sternly:

> I live by Truth, and from that I will not deviate.
> He who gathers up the waters in the sky, our father,
> the sun, and Sanjna, his wife,
> Are our parents. Between siblings such has not been
> done before
> And will never be done either.

This Yama is so pompous, thought Yami. Looking at him with her face raised, her eyebrows arched and her expression perky, Yami was ready with her reply:

> When even in the womb the Lord made us partners
> And His will reigns, no one violates His doing
> So the heavens and the earth know
> Partners we are and have always been.

Yami was sure she had found the clincher. When they had been together even in their mother's womb, why then object to togetherness now? She became bolder.

Yama sighed. His father had cursed his mother saying the daughter born to her would be of a restless mind. He should have known his sister would be whimsical. Here she was, true to the curse – building on a whim. And what irony that their elder brother Manu was called the law-giver for humankind. They were at two extremes, thought Yama. Since the birth of the twins, Sanjna was not just blinded by her dazzling husband but lived in great fear of him. One day, unable to bear his heat and light, she installed her shadow, Chhaya, in her place. She took an assurance from Chhaya that she would live and act as though she were Sanjna and answer to that name too. Sanjna then went away to her father's house.

When his wife no longer shut her eyes when he looked at her, unsuspecting Surya thought that all his remonstrations had had an effect. She bore him more children. But Manu, Yama and Yami soon sensed that Chhaya was kinder to her other children[7] than to them. In fact she was not nice to them. None of them knew she was not their real mother, though. They only noticed the partiality she showed towards the younger children. Manu was not perturbed by this differentiation on her part. Yama, however, bristled with indignation. Finally, one day he got so annoyed with her that he raised his leg to kick his mother. Chhaya got very angry, but instead of reprimanding the child, she cursed him saying, 'Your leg will fall off.' Surya overheard this, and when Yama complained to him that a mother would never curse her own children in such a manner, he agreed. 'This is not my mother,' said Yama. 'She has cursed me mercilessly.' The thought had occurred to Surya too. He soon found out the truth. Realising the wife by his side was not Sanjna, he set off on a search for her. When he found her and she confessed that his brilliance was too much for her to bear, he took immediate action. He asked Sanjna's father, Vishwakarma (Tvasthr), to pare down his radiance. Surya distributed the effulgence he had shed to many, including Agni (Fire). With his radiance shorn, his loving wife Sanjna returned to him.

Now that his happy family was back in place, Surya decided it was time to assign each of his sons their responsibilities. Manu he made the king of living beings. He then looked lovingly at Yama. He mitigated Chhaya's curse on him by saying the worms that fed on the wound on his legs, and not the leg itself, would fall to the ground. So Yama was saved from the curse and did not lose his leg.

This son of his was not just good-looking but also righteous. He knew right from wrong, and he was very just. He had the makings of a king – and king he should be, resolved Surya.

Yama was brought back to the moment when he saw Yami edge closer.

2

Yama and Yami

Yama moved away. He told Yami again in no uncertain terms that the celestials were watching. What would they say of such behaviour? Yami replied plaintively in a voice that seemed to stretch out to nab Yama as if to ensnare him:

> Who knows those early days of which you speak?
> Who has seen them? Who will tell us?
> You who define that which is moksha and that which is liberation, why do you fear Varuna and Mitra.
> I am besotted by you and wish to share your bed
> As a wife would surrender to her husband, I would to you
> Like the two wheels of a chariot, we can move together …

Yami was now becoming more assertive. What was Yama afraid of? His reasoning held no appeal for Yami. What did he know of the couples of yore? She asked him, 'Who has seen them? Who will tell us about their intimate moments anyway? O Yama, you have the power to control Mitra and Varuna and what they say, so why do you care if they are watching?'

Yama heaved a sigh of despair. Why would his sister not understand that the inseperables Varuna and Mitra[1] – Varuna, the all-embracing sky god, and Mitra, who brings men together – were upholders of rhta? Are they not invoked with the words 'Oblations to the eye of Mitra and Varuna, may every offering to these Gods be made in Truth'?[2] They respected him, Yama, only because he was a great follower of rhta, the cosmic order. If he himself were to disrupt the order, Varuna, Mitra and all his supporters as well as the superior deities would be thrown into cyclonic unrest and blind rage. Nothing misses Varuna–Mitra's eyes: they are said to have unwinking eyes and see the paths better than the human eye.[3] There would be no rhta. They would lose their sense of purpose and rootedness. It just required one act that went against the order to spread worldwide chaos. Such an act, once committed, could never be undone.

'Ssshhh!' said Yama rather loudly as he looked around, embarrassed. He hoped no one had heard her. He said firmly:

> The spies of the celestials who roam around close
> neither their eyes nor their ears

> They wander all around us watching: leave me and
> go quickly
> Oh wanton woman, to another with whom you can
> move like the chariot and the wheel.

Yami laughed. She looked around. The place was deserted. There was no one there but the two of them. He was overestimating the power of the celestials like Mitra and Varuna. Her brother was scared of what people would say. He was not unwilling, she concluded, and so persisted. He, Yama, was known as the one who knew right from wrong, and so he was afraid, afraid that his reputation would be tarnished. What was he so embarrassed about? Did he not know that Lopamudra, the great lady of dignity and piety, had brought her ascetic husband to bed with her when she so desired? Lopamudra's husband had committed to ascetic pursuits for life and was therefore practising celibacy. Her wait for him, day after day, seemed interminable, and she told him one evening, 'For several days and nights I have been serving you. Now I am growing older. It is time for you to turn your attention to me. Great gods who adhere to and live by Truth have also sought intimacy with their spouses.' Agastya, her husband, felt remorseful. 'Indeed,' he said, 'in pursuit of that very Truth I have spent my life in austerity.' He then accepted his wife's invitation.[4]

Yami whispered to herself, 'Great gods who adhere to and live by Truth also seek intimacy with their spouses ...' Why did Yama not understand this? If an ascetic could be moved, so could Yama, thought Yami, and emboldened, she became more provocative.

Yama was truly worried. He knew which way Yami's thoughts were going. He was sure Yami was thinking of Lopamudra and Rishi Agastya. The Agastya story was the gossip of their times. 'Yami, they were husband and wife,' Yama wanted to say. 'We are brother and sister.' He had to live up to his dharma as a brother.

Surya was very proud of Yama's adherence to dharma, to that which is right. If he were to hear this conversation, what would he think?

'You will be me, in another aspect. You will be my partner. I lead people while they live, you lead them after death,' Surya had told his son. 'Both of us are kala, or time. I make it, you keep it. You are the timekeeper.' Surya had appointed Yama as the guide to the netherworld, the path to which had not yet been carved. Yama would be the leader, the king, of the netherworld. This had been Surya's blessings for Yama. Yama's mind was therefore on something else, on becoming king of the netherworld.

Yami's loud voice interrupted his thoughts. Now she was trying to lure him by invoking Surya's blessings for Yama:

> 'Come, Yama,' she whispered.
> 'Come, Yama, do the act, even if it's unbrotherly.'

Yama realised that his warning that they were being watched by the celestials and that she would be put to shame were not enough to deter her. He wondered if he should call his dogs, Sharavara and Shyama. Yama laughed as he imagined their likely response. Though they liked Yami, they were bound to act on his behalf. They would perhaps chase Yami away. Yama was amused but did not want to subject his sister to such an experience.

Anyway, now was not the time to think of his hounds; Yami was taking his silence as consent. So he quickly changed his strategy and said:

> There will come in future times when brothers and sisters may commit acts that is not becoming of them
> O Subhage, that is not me. Dream of and look for another man and make your arm a pillow for him.

Yama was telling her that brothers and sisters would look for partners in unknown places and from families other than their own. But in future times there could be some who may act unbecomingly and commit incest. Yama was not one such. Yami too should change her mind in view of this and look for some other man who could fulfil her desires. Calling her the beautiful one, the auspicious one, the fortunate one – Subhage – Yama wanted her to realise that their love was of another kind. He was firmly showing her the right way, but not belittling her; instead he was complimenting her and addressing her respectfully.

But Yami was disgusted with his response. When there is yearning, it ought to be fulfilled. No reasoning is good enough. What is the use of a brother who is unable to fulfil the wishes of his sister! How sad is the situation when the sister is bereft of a husband even though she has a hale and hearty man next to her, so what if it is her own brother! And look at the brother, he has no offspring even though he has a woman beside him. 'I am very desirous, and so I say, come and let us meet in love,' said Yami. Yami was trying to tell Yama that he had no progeny. He will be known for posterity and his life would be complete only when he has a child.[5] Imagining that Yama must be grieving on that account, she offers, kindly, to remove her brother's angst.

What is the use of that brother who, despite being
 nearby, leaves his sister without a partner?
What is the use of that sister who, despite being
 nearby, cannot help remove her brother's angst?

Besotted in love I say these words to you, Come
close, and hold me in your tight embrace.

Yama refused.

I will not hold you close to my body in embrace:
when a brother comes close to a sister with such
intent, it is a sin
So look for someone other than me, prepare for
pleasures with another: your brother does not
desire this from thee, Subhage.

But merely being called Subhage could not make Yami happy. She required something else. She resorted to challenging Yama now. She called him a weakling. 'No man can tolerate this taunt,' thought Yami. 'I cannot understand why Yama would want some strange woman to cling to him as a creeper would to a tree or a girdle would around a horse,' thought Yami ruefully. Here she was all ready to embrace him.

It pains me to see that you are such a weakling
Indeed, I am unable to understand the workings of
your mind
As the lead rope binds a horse, as a creeper curls
around a tree
You want a strange woman to entwine her arms
about you?

What a weakling!

But Yama did not see this as a taunt. He realised there was no point in continuing the conversation. He ended the matter saying:

> Embrace another, Yami; let another take you in his arms, even as the honeysuckle rings the tree,
> You win his heart and let him win your fancy, and he shall form with you a great partnership.

Wishing her all the best in her hunt for a lover, Yama walked away.[6] Perhaps he should have done that a long time back, he thought.

There can be no references to time in this story – such as 'the next day' or 'the following afternoon'. Time did not exist. The sun never set, and there was no concept of time. Flowers never wilted, nor did birds stop flying, and trees bore fruit all the time. In such a world, Yami sat alone, wondering how to tackle Yama. Now he had left her and disappeared. She felt sorry for herself. After reflecting for a while, she decided to follow the path Yama had taken.

Hurriedly walking away from Yami's sight, Yama did not look back. He could feel Yami's eyes on him for quite some time though. But now he had come a long way ahead. The time had come, he thought, to fulfil his father's prophecy.

The courage to speak as she had came from Yami's belief that every man should ensure that his lineage carried on, he had to have progeny. Since Yama did not have any, Yami had 'offered her services', so to speak.

Yama did not need offspring. He who was Time himself lived in timelessness … there was no past, no present, no future. Yama could experience all three times at once. A story that was to be enacted later in time came to mind. It was when Parvati, Siva's consort, wanted a child and told Siva so.

> 'Why?' asked Siva. 'We are perfectly happy, and
> I am not a householder, nor am I going to die.
> The one who is not plagued by illnesses, why should
> he require medicines?
> Why do YOU want a child?
> The whole world is my creation.
> Sons are for householders to perform putrah
> pindaprayojanah (the last rites)
> And I, Siva, am imperishable.'[7]

Yama too was eternal: he was a celestial. He was destined to be king of a heaven which lay far beyond the sun. He was going to embrace death. He would never be a god, he would be king. The king of a realm that had yet to be explored. The time had come for him to proceed there. He had to choose to die. He could decide the time of his death.

Yami had lost sight of Yama. She kept calling out to him but got no response. Only her own voice seemed to echo back to her. She could now understand how King Pururavas must have felt. Pururavas was a king whose life was yet to unfold, but since Yami could see the past, present and future, she knew his story. There would be a king named Pururavas, a mortal. He would fall in love with an apsara, Urvashi, beautiful and charming. Urvashi would agree to marry him but on one condition – he should never intrude on her privacy when they were not making love. The agreement was honoured – until one day, when Urvashi was giving birth to their son and the king entered her chamber. Urvashi could not take that. The agreement had been transgressed. She bid adieu to the king, taking her son along with her. Pururvas was distraught. Urvashi, however, would not even look back as she walked away.[8]

But that happened in the world of mortals. Yami was sure she would not experience that. Yet she did.

She experienced the same sense of loss as Pururavas did, a certain emptiness ... was she imagining things? She had heard her father tell Yama that he would be a king. He had also called him 'restrainer of life'. She wondered what that meant.

Life at that time existed only in the celestial realm. Mortals had been conceptualised, but what would happen when their bodies gave way? Mortals would be created by the spread of Brahman Itself. It would manifest in individual abundance. Covering Its essence would be five layers. The outermost layer would be the *annamaya kosha*. This kosha, or sheath, would be built with anna, or food. The body would be formed by the semen and the egg, and then grow and develop with the intake of nourishing food. The next layer would be the *pranamaya kosha*, or the vital sheath, the prana or life force. Within that sheath would lie the *manomaya kosha*, the mental body, or that which holds the emotional body and mind. The fourth layer would be the *vijnanamaya kosha*, or that body which is responsible for cognition, intellect and wisdom. Finally, deep within would lie the *anandamaya kosha*, or the layer of bliss. Ensconced within all these five sheaths would be the Brahman, or Atman. The annamaya kosha, by definition, was perishable.

The sun, as Time, would ripen the grains on earth and produce food. Food would, in turn, be subject to decay. Perhaps, thought Yami, one could say that when the pranamaya kosha separated from or lost that link with the annamaya kosha, death would occur. The question that awaited a response was, what would happen after that disconnect? Where would the Atman go? Yami had heard Yama say that he would find a place where the Atman could rest before finding another womb for it to be born again as another embodied soul.

'Do not be foolish, Yama,' she had once admonished her brother. 'That means you will have to experience death. We are enjoying ourselves here.'

'Life is defined by death,' Yama had replied. 'Give up something of yourself for others.'

That was why Yami was always in fear of emptiness – that absence of Yama.

Suddenly, she saw a figure sprawled under a tree. She was not aware that another being existed on this island. Indeed, Yama had been correct, maybe this was a spy of Varuna's or Mitra's. She moved closer, cautiously. Holding her breath and standing on her toes, she tried to see who was lying on the grass and enjoying the beautiful weather. On getting still closer she found that it was Yama himself lying under the shade of the tree. She was delighted. Ah! It was not anybody else! Before he sat up, she would embrace him, she thought. She called out to him. He did not respond. Moving closer, she called out to him once more. Again there was no response. Then she shook him – maybe he was just ignoring her. But there was still no response.

Yami panicked. Yama was cold to the touch. 'Yama, Yama,' she screamed, her voice renting the skies. 'Answer me, Yama, I will not make any demands of you. Answer me, answer, answer, answer …'

Her voice was heard everywhere in the heavens. Surya took a deep breath. His son had taken the step, the significant life-creating step. Did the sun become a little dimmer? One could not tell because Yami's cries were penetrating every particle of the air, every cell of the mind of all the celestials, and that was the overarching experience. Almost all the celestials came to see death … how does it look when death claimed someone?

Yama was inert. Yama had died. He had withdrawn his prana, or breath, severing the connection with the annamaya kosha. This was the first death in the celestial realms. Yama would not respond to Yami any more.

Yami was inconsolable. She cried. She cried so much that her tears began to flow as a stream and swelled into a river. Soon the river threatened to flood the surroundings and her sorrow was all set to engulf the world. Everyone tried to console Yami, but she could not get over the loss. She continued to feel its immediacy, even after much time had passed.

Yama had died. The gods spoke to Yami to make her forget Yama.

Every time they spoke to her she said, 'Today he died.'

They said, 'So let's make night.'

Day existed at the time, but night didn't.

Then the gods created night.

Then the next morning came into being, there came a break in her thoughts.

She no longer felt the immediacy of Yama's death.

That is why it is said: 'Days and nights make someone forget a calamity.'[9]

That is how the gods decided to bring about a break in the day. They requested Sun to set and the world to be enveloped in darkness before he rose again. Thus there would be day and night. Yami would rest at night and cope better with her sorrow the following day. That turned out to be a good solution and Yami did get better, though her sorrow remained with her forever. When Sun set, he too immersed himself in thoughts of his brave son who had sacrificed himself for the creation of the world.

And with daytime and nighttime, Yama manifested as Kala, Time itself.

Yami then sang the right samans – songs that helped Yama ascend to the realms that lay beyond.[10] Anyone who recited the samans that Yami sang would be exalted in the heavens, it was later said. Having ensured that Yama ascended to heaven, Yami became the river Yamuna, for what Yama had told her reverberated in her mind: 'Give something of yourself for others.' She gave her waters to mortals all day, all night.

Yama was the first being to die. He was a celestial who embraced death. Sacrificing his life, he also became the creator of this world of mortals, father of Time, Time himself. If there was no death, there could be no life. Decay and degeneration are part of life. He died so that he could find the route to the netherworld. He had to find a place where people from the mortal world would come and rest before being reborn again in the world. That was the first sacrifice – giving a bit of oneself for a larger gain.

And so Yama went forth into unknown lands. Alone. Except for his two hounds, who joined him somewhere along the way.

Book 2

THE GENEROUS KING

3

Yama, the king

Yama was well settled in heaven. He also got married. Dhumorna was a good wife, hospitable to all who came to heaven. They had many children and one adopted daughter named Sunita. The name meant 'one who is well guided, well behaved, wise'. Through her he had a grandson, Vena.

How did Yama find the path to heaven? How did he get there? What were his trials and tribulations along the way, if indeed there were any? Did he perform yajna, as mortals do, to reach the heaven that he would rule? We do not know. Yama did not like to talk of his achievements. He never told anyone what transpired after his death. Having traversed an unknown path and reached the abode that would be his kingdom, he made it a beautiful and welcoming place for all the souls that came to rest there before being born on earth again. He was the guide, leader and protector of the netherworld. There were three heavens, two under the rule of Surya – or Savitr, as one form of Yama's father was called – and one under the reign of Yama.

Yama's kingdom was the highest, lying far beyond Surya's, in a direction between south and southwest. It was studded with diamonds all through and had four gateways. It was surrounded by high ramparts of more than a thousand yojanas.[1] It had beautiful gardens and parks, and birds of every imaginable hue. In every part of the city there were pretty maidens and choristers.

> There are three heavens up there
> two belong to Savitr, adjacent to each other
> Yama's world is the third, the home of heroes ...[2]

Great sages were living in the third heaven, in the court of Yama, and singing his praises. That is how Yama acquired the name Pitrapati, father of our ancestors. Yama could not be a god because he had died. But of all the kings, he was perhaps the most enviable, for he had a galaxy of wise men and sages in his court, attending to him. All the great men who trod the earth were now in heaven singing Yama's praises.

Yama's wife was gentle and good-natured. She is said to have risen from a funeral pyre. Her name, Dhumorna, carried the meaning of a shroud of smoke. She was wispy, like smoke, beautiful to behold and of the hue of a blue lotus. She carried her position of being the First Lady of the third heaven lightly. In fact, like her husband, she wanted to be the perfect host to all the great men and women who went from the mortal world to spend time in Yama's court. So she always carried in her left hand a twig from the matulanga[3] tree. Matulanga is a citrus fruit resembling a large lemon with a thick, green rind. It wards off ill health and its health benefits are equated to the gooseberry's.

Dhumorna accompanied Yama to all important events. They would ride Yama's buffalo, Mahisha, when they travelled. When Vishnu married Lakshmi, their wedding was a major event in the heavens. All the gods, decked in their best finery, went to attend the wedding. There Dhumorna met many other women, including Arundhati, Shandili and Lopamudra. They met in an extravagant hall, which had long rows of thousands of pillars embedded with jewels. It was dotted with many canopies of plantain trees under which the women sat and chatted. Many kalpatarus, or heavenly wish-yielding trees, offered their sweet, fragrant flowers to the gathering. Dhumorna, who loved her husband dearly, thought all those many bejewelled lamps of light still fell short of his resplendence. Elephants guarded the eight directions. All the rivers flowed in to fill the pots with their waters which the elephants raised with their trunks to shower down as ablution on the couple. Music and drums played, the moon shone brighter than ever and joy was in the air. Dhumorna caught her breath as she watched Lakshmi sitting on the throne and the wedding ceremony begin. Dhumorna was a romantic.

It was said that Yama acquired many more wives. Dhumorna could not care less. They all said many things. They even said Yama was always in the company of women and not a very serious being. Dhumorna paid no attention to such talk. She herself was called by many different names – Shyamala, the dark one, or Urmila. In some parts of the mortal world she came to be known as Aiyo. So much so that elders would tell their children, 'Hush! Do not say Aiyo, then Yama's wife will think you are calling her and Yama will come with her,' meaning death would come. Sushila and Hemamala were some of her other names.

There is a story of a mortal called Vijaya who is said to have seen Yama on earth. She was very scared at this, as all mortals fear death. But discovering Yama's good nature, she agreed to marry him. On her arrival at Yama's abode, he told her that she was free to do anything, but 'Do not ever venture into the southern quarter of the kingdom.'

Vijaya soon became convinced that she just had to go to the southern quarter. 'Maybe he has another wife,' she thought. On going there, she found many people suffering there, as that was hell. One among them was her own mother. She then asked Yama for her release. Yama told her that he had to have his count – if anyone was willing to fill in for her, he could let her go. Eventually they found someone and Vijaya got her mother released.

Dhumorna sighed. The story of Vijaya, which she too had heard, was born in a period when Yama was made the lord of naraka, or hell. When he got married to Dhumorna, he was the king who guided the dead to the land of peace and joy, called Yamapuri, where they rested till they were to be born again. He was not associated with torture, fear and hells as later mythologies tended to describe him. Vijaya was a character that emerged in these later times. That was why Dhumorna dismissed the story of Vijaya.

4
A day in Yamapuri

Every morning Yama was woken up with panegyrics in his heaven that was variously called Yamaloka, Yamapuri or Samyamanapuri. It was a unique city that shone brilliantly in the celestial realms. Mount Meru was considered the centre of the universe. It had five peaks and stood in the centre of Lake Manasa. To the southern side of Meru, lying within the periphery of Lake Manasa, was the abode of Lord Yama – Samyamanapuri. To the north of Meru, also on Lake Manasa, was the Vibhavari Nagari of Lord Soma. To the east of Meru, on Lake Manasa, lay Amravati, the golden city of Lord Indra. To the west of Meru, again on Manasa, was Lord Varuna's abode, Sukhanagari. If it was sunrise at Samyamanapuri it would be midday at Amravati; and if it was noon at Samyamanapuri it would be dawn at Sukhanagari, sunset at Amravati and midnight at Vibhavari.[1]

Welcoming sunrise and waking up their beloved king, the choristers in Samayamanapuri would sing thus:

Worship King Yama, son of Vivasvan, with your
offerings
He who leads us mortals to our destination together
Yama carved out this route for us, a route on which
no one can stop us
A route that he makes easy, along which our
forefathers have travelled.
With the help of Kavyas, Angiras, Brhaspati and
Rkvans, our forefathers, Yama forges ahead
While gods and all celestials also join in worship,
with praise or offerings.

The whole city would resound with the panegyrics. It was customary to wake up a king with panegyrics. Did the ones being sung in Samyamanapuri sound more intense and did they touch the heart more than the panegyrics sung in any other kingdom? There was a reason for that. All those who sang, all those who worshipped Yama, thought of their forefathers who were sitting in Yama's court, living in his city. They, their forefathers, had followed the path shown by Yama. The worshippers were therefore very keen on keeping the king happy so that he in turn is kind to his people. Inviting him to be present when they make their offerings to him, they almost compete with each other to offer their salutations to him.

O Yama, who is in the company of Angiras and others,
Do honour us by coming and sitting on this seat of
kusha grass for the yajna
May the passages invoking you, as composed by the
great sages, please you
And may you be happy with this prayer
Arriving with all Angirases in different forms,
gladden the heart of the yajaman (master of
ceremonies).
I will request your father Vivaswan to come too so
that he may further encourage the priest.
Angirases, Navagvas, Atharvans and Bhrgus[2]
deserve to be offered Soma
May they bless us, and with their grace may we
attain to good and auspicious ends.[3]

The choristers were seeking the blessings of Yama for themselves as well as for the mortals performing the yajna on earth. They were all there in Yama's heaven – Angiras, Atharvan, Bhrgu, the architect sages of yore. It was an exalted court over which Yama presided.

Mortals were told not to worry about death, for Yama would be waiting to receive them in his wonderful abode, with music and peace and the company of exalted souls. The panegyrics being sung to wake up the King of Death, enjoying the position of a god, were pleasing to the ears. They now addressed the travellers on their way to Yama's kingdom, saying:

> On this very same ancient path, our forefathers have travelled,
> Come on, speed forth, and go ahead to the land where
> On reaching you will both Yama and Varuna meet.
> Meet Yama, meet your ancestors and the rewards of your meritorious actions,
> Discard evil and wrongdoing and don a brilliant, subtle body, radiant and glorious.
> Shoo! Turn away, all evil spirits, this place is not for you
> With light and water and restful nights
> Comfort has been provided to our ancestors by Yama.

Yamapuri was indeed a new dwelling. Identified by Yama and developed by Vishwakarma. The earth was under the reign of his father, Surya. Yama ruled Yamaloka, where goodness alone reached. Yama's two hounds were with him. The hymns praise them too. Motivating the travellers to come forth with speed and enthusiasm, the singers go on to say:

> Come on, race Yama's watchmen, Sarama's sons,
> The two dogs who walk along this path
> Then you will quickly meet your ancestors
> who are enjoying in the company of Yama

And to Yama, the verse implores:

> O Yama those two four-eyed dogs that you have
> Which watch over men and guard the pathway
> Bid them to take care of these travellers
> On whom you too should bestow your kindness
>
> These dark coloured dogs with distended nostrils
> Who are your messengers that roam amongst people
> May they ensure for all of us and the travellers
> A fair existence and enable us to see the light of
> the sun

The two dogs were Sharavara and Shyama. They were the offspring of Sarama, who was King Indra's hound. Shyama, as the name implies, was black in colour. Sharavara, also called Sabala, was spotted. Their father was Sisira, who was believed to be a demon. The two hounds have also often been described as *mithudrsa*, or those who could not see or appear together at the same time. They saw alternately, implying thus that they complemented each other. That is why they are also called Yama's day and night guardians. They are described as having four eyes each. To Yama this description did not sound strange or abnormal in any way. One pair of eyes observed the mortal world. The other guarded the gates to Yamapuri and directed the souls along the right path. Yama winced at how the description of his dogs had undergone changes over time. They had started being described as bloodthirsty hounds, who the people said were deeply influenced by Sisirama, the demon whose name implies he was a combination of Sisir and Sarama. His dogs were actually gentle creatures, loyal and honest.[4]

But before turning to the changes that came about with time, there is more to know of the initial days of Yama in his heaven. Agni was his great friend and adviser. One panegyric goes on to say:

> To Yama pour the Soma, bring to Yama consecrated gifts:
> To Yama the sacrifice prepared and heralded by Agni goes.

Though it may be well to remember this too:

> They call him Indra, Mitra, Varuna, Agni,
> And he is heavenly winged Garuda.
> To what is One, sages give many a title,
> They call it Agni, Yama, Matarisvan (Agni).[5]

There was only One. They, Indra, Mitra, Varuna, Agni, Garuda, Yama, Matarisvan (again, Agni), were all one, for their source was the same. Yet they performed different duties. Agni carried prayers and offerings from the mortal world to the world of the dead. He was thus Yama's close collaborator and friend. Surya had stationed his son Yama in the south. Yama is considered one of the dikpalas[6] in mythology and is the dikpala of the south. Agni is the dikpala of the southeast. So they were neighbours too.

The idea was that Agni, who is the source of all – the fire that exists as the sun in the sky, the lightning in the atmosphere and the fire on earth – is unifying, bringing together, gathering, all the mortals and the immortals. To please Yama, the only way to ward off death, Agni is the only means. Without Agni no sacrifice can be performed, no gods appeased.

However, Yama always held that true intent and righteous character stood way above rituals. Sacrifice, as Yama had himself shown, was the way to betterment. Neither fire nor priests were required for sacrifice. Sincere intent alone was the key. Yama recollected a hymn that was chanted as part of the rituals performed for the dead. The hymn went:

O cruel Death, into your fiery mouth
I offer the sacrifice of my efforts and comfort
For the freedom of these unfortunates who are
  bound to be caught in your grip
Although these unfortunates believe that you
  (Death) is their destiny by birth,

I know that you are Death only because of sheer
want of will, intelligence and action,
You are not the destiny.[7]

Yama understood that power of moral rectitude was not easy to attain and that Agni, whom the priests implored to guide on the journey from this world to the other, was often the purifier, even of intent, and so played the major role in the communication with Yama through offerings made by mortals.

5

Yama and Agni

Yama, Varuna, Mitra and Agni were friends, each performing his duty to keep rhta, the cosmic order. But nothing is simple, and even these celestial beings have their share of reluctance to live a life of responsibility.

One day Agni disappeared. Everyone was in a fix. Where were they to find Agni? How would they conduct any sacrifice? A search party was constituted. Among them were Vayu, who was all-pervading and so had a good chance of locating Agni; Mitra, because he was friendly and in harmony with the infinite (and so brought about order, or rhta); and Yama, the god of the underworld, or the dark part of consciousness. Anyway, they were the only three major powers of those times, apart from Agni himself. They were gods of friendship, harmony, integrity and order among humans. Varuna was the lord of the sky and the cosmos, and the enforcer of morality and truth.[1] Yama was Dharma himself. He embodied morality, truth and order.

Agni was found by Yama, hiding under a dark blanket-like mass under water. It turned out he did not want to shoulder the responsibility of being the chief communicator between earth and heaven. So he was literally hiding so that no one could find him. Now Yama had found him, as Yama always finds those who try to hide themselves in their own darkness.

They had searched everywhere, high and low, in all the ten directions, it is said. It was important that they found Agni. But the search went on for some time before Yama spotted his effulgent being. The conversation that ensued was as follows:

> That was a rather large offering that wrapped itself
> around you
> Hiding within which you entered the waters
> O Jatadeva Agni, one celestial deity saw all your
> forms, even though in hiding.

Agni had been found hiding under waters. Jataveda, which means all-knowing, is an epithet for Agni. Coming out of hiding, Agni asked:

> Tell me, Varuna and Mitra, who saw me? Who was the deity who found me? Who was the deity who saw all my forms so clearly? If he has seen me, tell me, where lie all the sacred logs of Agni that lead him to God?

The search party replied:

> O effulgent one whose brilliance radiates everywhere
> We looked for you in the waters and amongst
> vegetation.
> Then Yama found you, god of brilliant splendour,
> wonderful even in your secret dwelling.

Was Agni unhappy to be found?

Why did you hide, why did you run away, they asked Agni.

Agni, the most powerful, who gives warmth, helps food ripen and can also burn everything down to ashes, said nervously:

> O Varuna, afraid of having to perform my duties
> during sacrificial worship,
> I entered the waters so that the gods would not be
> able to find me
> Seeking refuge in this manner, my several forms got
> scattered in the waters,
> Hiding wherever they could. I do not accept this job
> of being the messenger during sacrifices.

The story goes that Agni had three brothers: Bhoopati, Bhuvanapati and Bhutapati. They had all been engaged in the same work for which Agni was now being coerced by Yama, Varuna and Mitra. Among other tasks laid out before them during a yajna, they had to carry the offerings and deliver them to the respective deities to whom they had been offered. While performing this laborious task, Agni's three brothers had lost their lives.[2] So the fourth, Agni, containing the fire, went into hiding. 'I cannot bear that burden,' said Agni, of being the one to carry the sacrifices for men and mortals.

The three deities cajoled him to return. 'Come, Agni,' they said, 'make the pathways that lead to God. You are the only one who can.' Agni was reluctant. After all, that was why he had run away. Unfortunately, Yama had found him, as none could escape Yama. And now all three of them were forcing him to undertake that onerous task. They tried to reassure him and cheer him on. 'No harm will come to you. On the contrary, you will be immortal,' they said. 'You are mighty now, you will become almighty when you accept this role,' they told him. Eventually they managed to convince him, and Agni, reluctantly and out of compulsion, went with them. Everyone sang praises of Agni, the life-giving force. Agni sought the boon of a long life by asking that the best of the offerings should be given to him. The three of them, Varuna, Mitra, and Yama, replied:

> O Agni! Not a part but the whole offering will be to
> you and you only

Not just that, the regions in all four directions will
humbly salute you.[3]

Even though it was Yama's keen eye that had spotted Agni, Yama felt a kinship with Agni. He understood how difficult and burdened Agni felt as he meted out equal treatment to all. Once Yama had gone through a similar experience, that is, he had stopped working. He had not gone into hiding, but his absence from duty had caused panic, and havoc too.

Many celestials had gathered in the Naimisaranya and were performing a great yajna. Yama too was enthused. As he had always only received offerings, he was drawn to the idea of participating in a yajna. So he attended the ceremony, and then got so engrossed in it that he lost count of time. As a result, no one died. The number of human beings increased greatly. So Soma, Indra, Varuna and other gods went to Brahma to complain about the frightening increase in the number of human beings. 'Why do you worry? You are immortal,' Brahma said, laughing. 'But, O Lord, even the mortals are now becoming immortal,' they replied. Brahma assured them that Yama would sweep away a large number once he was finished with the yajna.[4] So they all urged Yama to finish the yajna quickly and return to office! When Yama did, he caused a natural calamity to happen, and indeed many lives were swept away, bringing order back to earth.

To Yama, Agni was more than a friend and guide. Agni was called Pavaka, sacrifice; Hutasana, or one who accepts all sacrificial offerings; and Jvalana, one who is always glowing. Some said he was his father's brother; others said he was the seed and that Surya was born of him ... it never became clear to Yama, but whatever the truth Yama knew he depended on Agni to continue his communication with the mortal world. Their connection was very close. Agni was selfless. He accepted material sacrifices that are conventionally made at all yajnas and brought them straight to Yama.

> To Yama sacrifice is prepared and through Agni it goes.
> Offer to Yama holy gifts enriched with butter, and draw near:
> So may he grant that we may live long days of life among the gods.
> Offer to Yama, to the king, oblation very rich in meath:
> Bow down before the rsis of the ancient times, who made this path in days of old.

> Into the six expanses flies the Great One in Trkadrukas.
> The Gayatri, the Trstup, all meters in Yama are contained.[5]

With that the daily panegyrics would come to an end. The learning was that there was and is only One. The great One. The supreme. The infinite. The omnipotent. It is this One that vibrates, rules and pervades the multifariousness of existence through three dimensions of time – past, present and future; six seasons of the year – spring, summer, the rains, autumn, mild winter and severe winter; three regions of space – heaven, earth and the firmament; and six directions – up, down, north, south, east and west. Trishtubh, Gayatri and other Chhandas abide in the one word, Om, as all orders of matter, energy and thought abide in the infinite Shakti of Om. And all these orders of omniscience, omnipresence and omnipotence abide in One, emerge from That and converge into That: Yama, the ordainer.

And the choristers would offer their worship saying:

> Yama is far, very far indeed. Vivasvan, the sun, relatively, is close. Beyond Yama, I see nothing, nothing that I know. My yajna of love, devotion and non-violent self-sacrifice is established in Yama, and really it is the self-refulgent Yama who has spread the light of the sun also over the regions of the universe.[6]

The panegyrics over, Yama would be ready to begin the day. His courtiers would be waiting for him.

Today, as he stepped out, his wife Dhumorna came to chat with him. 'Listen to what people are saying,' she was saying.

'I do not really want to know now. You know it is nothing new,' Yama replied.

'Living in denial, eh, Granddad?' Vena, son of Sunita, shouted, as he walked past.

Yama cringed at this. Dhumorna admonished Vena with a ssshhh … but Vena had gone by then.

Book 3

THE FEARFUL ENDER

6

Yama and Markandeya

'Yesterday,' began Dhumorna, 'a priest who had exhausted his time on earth and was therefore here seemed to have spoken to some people here. He said he wanted to see you. When asked why, he said he wanted to catch a glimpse of your green face, large teeth and horns. The people got annoyed with him, but he begged for forgiveness and told them of the legend that was doing the rounds on earth. He said that you, Yama, used to be very proud of your looks and that you spent your time frolicking with maidens who were falling for you. Is that true, Yama?' asked Dhumorna.

'Come on, Dhumorna, I have more important things to attend to,' said Yama, walking past her.

But Dhumorna stopped him as she had more to say. 'He also said that you, distracted by these many beautiful women, were not attending to your duties properly. This complaint reached Siva, and he summoned you to Kailasha. Siva asked you why people were not scared of you any more on earth and suggested that you had far too many fair friends, in the celestial realms as well as on earth. That is why your work is being neglected. You laughed it away, saying none of that was true, but Siva was not convinced.

'Then Siva asked you to go to a pond nearby and fetch him some water. You went in all earnestness. There you saw a terrifying face in the waters which was of a distasteful colour, had a huge moustache, a red tongue and uneven teeth. The figure had horns on its head. Yama, you were scared. You thought you had seen a monster. You rushed back to tell Siva that there was a strange creature in the pond. Now it was Siva's turn to laugh and you felt he was laughing at you and your angst. You hadn't realised that you had seen your own reflection. You begged Siva to restore your looks. To no avail. So you went to Brahma and Vishnu, seeking their help. Nothing changed. Vishnu was a little compassionate and removed your horns.'[1]

Dhumorna looked at Yama indignantly. Yama smiled. 'Don't worry. You know the truth. Do I look like that?'

'Of course not!' said Dhumorna.

'Then why do you worry? Few try to get close to Truth. Those who do know that I am an aspect of Siva. I am part of Him. These knowledgeable ones reach here. Since only a few seek such knowledge, we have fewer people coming here these days. They do not manage to cross the Vaitarani.[2] The priest must be an exception. Those who do come do not go back and tell, isn't that so? So we will have to put up with such rumours. Our lives are shrouded in mystery. The mortal world recognises only that which appears before it under the light of the sun. We are on the other side, and therefore difficult to be known,' Yama told his wife lovingly. Though Dhumorna was not convinced, she was happy that her handsome, soft-spoken Yama was unperturbed.

But Yama was actually distracted … he had a job at hand.

There lived a sage called Mrikandu, whose wife's name was Mrduvati. The pious couple were happy but had one regret. They had no children. So they prayed to Siva for offspring. After long years of prayer, one day Siva Himself appeared before them to grant them a boon. 'You shall have a child, but choose if you want a hundred long-lived but foolish sons or one wise one with a short lifespan of sixteen years.'

Mrikandu chose to have one wise child, even if he would live only sixteen years. The son, named Markandeya, could recite the sacred texts from a very young age and was very wise. For the first few years after his birth the parents were very happy, but later they were fraught by the thought that Markandeya's death was getting closer. In his sixteenth year, they could no longer control their sorrow. Markandeya wondered why his parents were both so sad. He was keen to know and his father told him why. 'Do not worry,' he told his father. 'Siva will take care of me.'

The appointed hour came and Yama's two messengers appeared, ready to yank the life out of Markandeya. But Markandeya sat embracing a Siva linga and praying to the Lord. He was chanting the Mrtyunjay mantra:

> Oṃ tryàmbakaṃ yajāmahe sugándhiṃ puṣṭi-
> várdhanam |
> urvārukám iva bándhanān mṛtyó murkṣīya mā́
> 'mṛ́tāt ||[3]

Now Yama himself reached the place and called out to Markandeya. He knew the boy was in prayer. But he was bound by the fact that Siva Himself had given this child only sixteen years on earth. So he was compelled to throw his noose, which fell on the linga and caused Siva to manifest. Siva, pleased with Markandeya's devotion, granted him release from Yama.[4]

When Yama returned to Yamapuri, Dhumorna was waiting, looking anguished. 'Oh! I am so glad to see you. They told me you were dead. Since the whole world looked still for a while, I got very worried,' she said tearfully.

'You too, you foolish girl,' guffawed Yama. Dhumorna looked at Yama bemused, trying to understand what he meant. 'Can the dead be killed?'

And Dhumorna too burst out laughing. 'Why do they say that then?' she asked.

'Let me tell you what happened,' said Yama. 'When Markandeya was born, Siva had given him a lifespan of only sixteen years. Now, he was so impressed with Markandeya that he felt he should extend his life and listen to his prayers. Siva manifested in all his aspects, and you know I am an aspect of Siva, so I merged into him. When I became one with him, it stopped decay and destruction. He had enveloped time. That is why I am called Kala also. Everything came to a standstill, which meant he held time. When he held time, no one aged, no one died, no one was born, and everything stopped. He could not take back his prophecy that Markandeya would live only sixteen years. Instead, he stopped time itself.

'But that was not a good solution. Everything everywhere stopped and life could not progress. People beseeched Siva to restore time. Siva realised he had to take action. He granted timelessness to Markandeya, and he withdrew the hold on time for the rest of the world. He returned to Kailasha. I was thus detached from him, and I too have returned. When Siva appeared, I naturally did not have a separate existence, I was subsumed into his. Markandeya alone will live in timelessness, which means he will always be sixteen years of age.'

After assuaging Dhumorna, Yama retired to his room and mused over the many changes of the past few centuries. In the beginning there was just a few of them, Indra, Agni, Varuna, Mitra and Yama, and Yama's father, Surya. Yama was then considered a benevolent king whose kingdom lay far beyond even the sun. The sun was closer than Yama's kingdom. It was essential to know how to get to his kingdom. Yama made the path. He was cordial and looked after his guests with care before they returned to earth for their next birth. But many things happened thereafter.

Mortals on earth now started travelling its length and breadth. Different beliefs and cultures had developed in the different parts of the world. Cultures interacted. People who believed time was linear came into contact with people who knew time was cyclical. The former viewed physical death and mortality as the final end and not as a continuous journey towards perfection of the soul. That brought fear of the end, distress and sorrow into their lives. When such people came into contact with people who had grown up knowing time was cyclical, ideas started intermingling. As the mystery that lay beyond the sun was impenetrable for the average human, the argument that death was the end seemed to gradually gain more popularity. Yama felt that that was when death as we understand it today came to be. Until then, immortality was viewed as changing from one birth to another. Now it became one birth, one life, and death as the end, and Antaka, another name for Yama – meaning the one who brings matters to an end – brought life to an end.

Added to this was another change. Mortal life had been thought of as consisting of creation, decay and destruction. But very often earthly beings indulged in destruction before any decay took place. Thus, rhta, or order, could no longer be maintained. Slight disapproval was punishment enough in earlier days, but now even a strong reprimand had no effect, and imprisonment and killing were becoming more common. With destruction gaining ground, the onus of every human action needed to be pinned down. The responsibility shifted from a superior external power to within oneself. Each individual became responsible for his or her own actions. In the Vedic times, sacrifice[5] was a means of ensuring a smooth passage to the other world. It had also been thought of as the only way to gain release from the chains of rebirth. Now, with the advent of the Jaina school of thought, Buddhist school of thought and the Upanishadic period, the doctrine of reincarnation had gained popularity, and so a good heart and righteous actions were the tests of qualifying for ultimate release. This meant that for every action, there was a binding karma. Different actions resulted in different types of karma. Many permutations and combinations were required to accommodate all kinds of people who erred in all kinds of ways. Each kind of offence resulted in different punishments and results, and so Yama found hells being added to his empire every day.

Today there are many hells, mused Yama. He had set up only the beautiful place of Samyamanapuri. But now very few people came here. Thieves went to the naraka or hell named Tamisaram; those who cheated on their spouse went to Andhatamisra. One who did not respect his or her parents went to Kalasutram. The count rose from one to four to twenty-one to finally twenty-eight hells in the last count.[6] It may also be clearer now why Dhumorna did not pay much heed to the story of Vijaya that people were telling each other. These stories were told primarily to emphasise the torture that the hells held for them and the possibility that they could end up there if they did not lead a righteous life.[7]

The result of all this was that death itself was seen as a frightening beginning to afterlife punishment for the wrongs committed in one's life, and so the more terrible Yama looked, the easier it was to convey the message.

In the earlier Vedic days, mortals departed from the mortal world and traversed to the land of Yama, and rested or bided time there till they returned to the mortal world. Yama, the first mortal, the pathfinder who leads the soul after death, benevolent ruler of the afterlife, regarded with reverence as a guide to souls, was associated with peaceful transition to the afterlife. He was a wise and virtuous figure rather than a punisher or a fearsome deity who is prayed to for a peaceful afterlife. This was his image in the Vedas. Now in the Upanshadic times and the epic-Puranic age Yama had become something like a fearful monster!

Stories like Markandeya's and Svetha Muni's reinforced this idea. People started hating Yama, who they felt was the cause of their end. As we saw earlier, Yama came to be called Antaka, or the one who brings life to an end, which was death. And the only escape from this was through devotion, as Markandeya's had wrought. This story became a motif, and many such began to be told. One of them was the story of the sage Svetha.

7
Yama as Antaka

In a cave high in the mountains lived a sage named Svetha. He was a devout follower of Siva and worshipped him all the time. He was now quite old. One day Yama mounted Mahisha and came to his doorstep.

Rishi Svetha, being quite evolved spiritually, could see that Kala or Yama was approaching him. He was not worried. 'O Tryambakeswara!' he called out to Siva. The he sat back calmly, thinking, 'Who can harm me when Siva is taking care of me?'

Yama smiled, reading his thoughts and hearing him call out to Siva. 'Who can help you now? When the time comes, no one can save you,' declared Yama.

Svetha eyes filled with tears. He did not want to die. He said, 'What can you do when my Lord Siva is by me! Better leave and stop behaving in such a manner with Siva's devotees.'

Yama did not like to be challenged. He waited for a moment, then wound Svetha up in his noose and said a little arrogantly, 'Now let us see who helps you.' Yama was one who went by rules. That was how he had to function. He could not heed recommendations from anyone.

So Siva had to manifest himself. And when he did, Yama lost his independent identity. Rishi Svetha was saved. Siva went away, and with him Yama too went away.

Rishi Svetha thought Siva had killed Yama. So did everyone else. But Yama emerged from Siva when they left the place and each went his own way.

Yama had become a punitive figure in the Epic and Puranic periods, picturised as carrying a noose (pasa) and wielding a club (danda), and of course fearsome to behold. Mortals and celestials were now more distant from each other. In earlier times, sages and rishis themselves knew the secret of immortality and this was not read as a 'defeat' of Yama.

There was once a sage named Dadanc.[1] He knew how to fix a head that had been severed from the body and bring the being back to life. The Ashvins, the divine twin horsemen and physicians of the gods, approached Rishi Dadanc to gain knowledge of the secret of *madhu vidya*, the highly sacred and esoteric knowledge of immortality and unity of existence. However, there was a complication.

Lord Indra, king of the gods, had warned Dadanc not to reveal this secret knowledge to anyone, threatening that his head would burst into a thousand pieces if he did. But the Ashvins pleaded with Rishi Dadanc as they deeply desired this knowledge for the benefit of the world.

Dadanc eventually agreed to share the madhu vidya with them but devised a clever plan to outwit Indra. Before revealing it to the Ashvins, he told them to cut off his head and replace it with the head of a horse. Using this temporary form, he imparted the sacred knowledge to the Ashvins. The horse head shattered into a thousand pieces. The Ashvins replaced the horse head with the original head, reviving Rishi Dadanc. Thus the sage upheld both his promise to Indra and his duty to share his secret knowlededge.

This knowledge was to be found not just among sages and rishis. Even kings – the evolved ones – had this knowledge. Svethaketu, son of Uddalaka Aruni, a highly respected sage, once appeared in the court of King Pravahana Jaivali, who asked him, 'Do you know how beings depart hence at death?'

'No, Your Majesty,' replied Svethaketu.

'Do you know the way of the fathers and the way of the gods?'

'No, Your Majesty,' replied Svethaketu.

King Jaivali asked Svethaketu many more questions along this strain, none of which Svethaketu knew the answer to.

Svethaketu then returned home and asked his father the same questions. The father too had to admit he did not have the answers. So both now came to the king and sought his guidance. The king told them that this knowledge was known only to kings, not even to priests.[2]

The story of Dadanc reminded Yama of a children's story based on a similar idea. Vishnu Sharman, a priest, was appointed teacher of three princes, sons of the king of Mahilaropya. Eschewing the traditional way, Vishnu Sharman taught them through the medium of stories. One story he told them was about four friends who wanted to go out into the wide world to earn their fortune. Three are well trained in the sastras while the fourth is unlettered. Initially the three educated friends were reluctant to take the fourth along, thinking he would be a burden on them. 'Kings honour only the knowledgeable. So we will have to share our earnings with him,' they said. But eventually one of them convinced the other two that they should not be petty.

En route they saw the carcass of an animal. They saw in it an opportunity to show off their knowledge. One of the three educated friends said he could assemble the bones. The second said he could cover the skeleton with skin, and the third said he could breathe life into the animal. So eager were they to test their prowess that they ignored the unlettered friend's protests. 'This is the carcass of a lion, do not bring it to life,' he said. But the three brought it back to life, and the lion feasted on the three knowledgeable men. The fourth escaped as he had climbed a nearby tree.[3]

Yama reflected that immortality was viewed as product of learning. That is why Goddess Saraswati, the goddess of learning, was always propitiated along with Yama so that one's learning may be complete. When learning was incomplete, as in the case of the three friends in the story, it resulted in disaster. Learning was complete if the Truth that all is One was understood. With such learning, action is undertaken for the larger good and not for flaunting one's ego. Dadanc used his knowledge for the larger good. But the three friends who brought the lion back to life were showing off their learning. The arrogance of learning, reflected Yama, can be blinding.

All these stories highlight one aspect or other of true knowledge. And what does true knowledge reveal? That there is no death. Only the body decays. For the soul to acquire a new body, Yama provides the resting room. So Yama is no enemy. He is the benevolent king of the highest heaven.

When death came to be viewed as the end, human aspiration to be immortal was challenged greatly. Ritual, secret knowledge of evolved sages and rishis and proximity with the celestials were replaced by the doctrine of karma, which became central to Yama's role as perceived by the mortals. Though both schemes admitted of the cyclical nature of life, Yama became a punitive figure in the latter, one believed to judge souls based on their karma, determining whether they would be sent to hell, reincarnated or attain liberation (moksha). His role was no longer simply to guide the dead to the afterlife but to evaluate their actions and administer appropriate punishment or reward. So much so that once Garuda asked to know what lay beyond, in the realm of Yama. How the cruel are punished and how the noble find their way. This knowledge was passed down by Vishnu Himself when he told Garuda about Yama and his ways, in what is known as the *Garuda Purana*. In this text and in some others too, imagination runs riot describing the physical structure of the various hells added to Yama's empire and the tortures Yama metes out to the evil in hell. Texts like the *Garuda Purana*[4] were revised and rewritten over time to describe the kinds of tortures that await the human being who does not live a life of rectitude.

Whatever the perception of Yama through the ages, his deeply philosophical nature was retained as one of his characteristics from the Vedic period. From being considered a wise king he was now called the knower of Brahman. During the second and third centuries CE, when the later mythological sections of the epics and the Puranas were being composed, when religious activity and cerebral interpretations of religion were at their peak, the understanding of the people went through dynamic changes.[5] The idea of an ishta devata, or a personal god, emerged, as also the idea of different people following different gods. The trinity of Brahma, Vishnu and Siva became the most popular and powerful of the gods. The triad was worshipped with pujas and other rituals. Sacrifices were no longer the order of the day. Siva embodied much of the power and role of Yama. And Siva was more. Yama remained the king of death. In order to build faith in the new triad of Siva, Brahma and Vishnu, stories such as the one about Rishi Svetha began to be circulate.[6]

Even though such stories of devotion gained great popularity, another story that was also told during those times emphasised the importance of Yama.

Once Vishnu, as Krishna, tried to play the role of Yamaraja. This was during treta yuga, when Krishna had assumed the duties of Yama. A sage called Lomasha once told Yudhishthira, the eldest of the Pandavas:

> O great one! When the God of Gods started
>   performing the duties of Yama
> There was no death on earth but there were
>   innumerable births
> Birds, beasts, deer and every other animal multiplied
> O foremost of men! By this massive increase in beings
> The earth began to sink down a thousand yojanas.

Earth was so burdened that she had to go to Vishnu Himself and ask for redressal. 'Do not worry,' Vishnu told her, 'I will repair the situation.' With that promise, Vishnu had to incarnate as a boar (Varaha) and dive deep into the ocean and bring up Mother Earth.[7] Soon Yama resumed his duties, for without him there was chaos.

Changes, changes, changes! Even Chitragupta, Yama's accountant, was a later addition. His role was to keep the karmic accounts. So he is worshipped everywhere on earth, hoping that if he was pleased, he would balance the right side enumerating their good deeds and the left enumerating their bad deeds and they would not suffer in a hell!

Yama smiled at the thought of balancing out good and bad deeds. One thought led to another and he started laughing heartily. Had anything really changed in the world? The hope was that if devotion was heightened and fear of the afterlife intensified, people may be brought on the path of rectitude. The promise, if such behaviour was adhered to, was the boon of immortality. The Mrtyunjay mantra in essence is a prayer to Siva to keep us detached from the world:

> I worship that effervescent Siva of three eyes, the
> one who nourishes us.

> As from its stem the cucumber is separated, falls off, so too may I be released from death and connected to my source.[8]

Yama snapped his fingers and smiled to himself. Did people realise that when you became one with the source, there would be no you?

Yama walked on …

Book 4

THE COMPASSIONATE TEACHER

8

Dhumorna waits for Yama

Dhumorna was restless. She had been waiting three days and three nights for him. She was still in bed, the day had not dawned. She was tossing about thinking of all the things she had to do that day. Suddenly, she woke up with a jolt. So much light! The day must have dawned. She looked out and, brilliant as the sun, it was her husband Yama riding home. The sun had not yet risen. The sun's son, Yama, was travelling across the skies. Dhumorna felt a surge of excitement now that Yama was finally coming back home.

Every time Dhumorna beheld him, she could not help but smile … he looked so gorgeous, her husband. Tall and magnificent, he looked even more attractive because his skin was dark and shining. When he smiled, it was such a kind and loving smile! Did he know he was good-looking and so dressed with care to accentuate his appearance? Dhumorna giggled. He generally wore clothes that were either golden or red. His choice of ornaments was exquisite. His ear ornament, like two globes, were sparkling next to his cheeks. He had four arms. In his right hands he held a mace and a rod, the danda. In one of his left hands he held a shield. With the other, thought Dhumorna shyly, he would embrace her and place her on his lap.[1] Now that he was riding Mahisha, his buffalo, he was holding the reins in that hand.

As she pictured her husband sitting on his throne, her thoughts could be put in verse:

> There, the Lord of Justice, on an auspicious and
> unparalleled throne
> Spread over ten yojanas and embellished with every
> possible gem
> Sits, the noblest best, with an umbrella over his head
> Prosperous, adorned with earrings, wearing a diadem
> And more beautiful ornaments all, splendid like a
> blue cloud
> With beautiful maidens fanning him with hand fans[2]

A man of such grandeur, such splendour was He, who showed mortals the path to heaven.

Soon everyone in Yamapuri could see him and hear the bells on the neck of his buffalo. Celebrating his return, the bards of the kingdom started singing his praises:

> Worship King Yama, son of Vivasvan, with your
> offerings

The voices of the bards resonated in the air as Dhumorna adjusted her clothes and hair in preparation to meet her husband.

Dhumorna wondered how people could spread rumours about Yama being so grotesque to look at when he was so very handsome! But, sighed Dhumorna, how many people saw him? They came here only after death. They feared him so much on earth that they spread many stories about him in ignorance. What Dhumorna did not realise was that different people saw him in differently. Rather, he appeared differently to different people. The good and righteous saw him as splendrous and magnificent. When the righteous go to the kingdom of the dead, Yama himself comes to greet them. When they see Yama, they see someone who has a close resemblance to Vishnu with a conch and a discus in one pair of hands and a sword and a mace in the other. He is gentle and kind to them.[3] Those mortals who have not been able to take the name of the Lord even once in their lifetime face Yama's intolerance. Such people, it is said, see the terrible form of Yama. In order to create fear in people, Yama was described as roaring and angry, seated on a buffalo, with thirty-two hands. His eyes are deep-set and red. His nose long and his mouth with sharp, protruding fangs ... The weapons he carries glitter in the sun, making them look even sharper than they are. Even Chitragupta, it is said, is scared to behold his master in this form.[4]

Yama could see Dhumorna rushing out of the house to meet him. She is up early, he thought.

But now something else was occupying his mind. Generally, when he returned from his tours, he looked forward to observing his kingdom from afar. He could not help but admire its beauty and splendour. He got the chance to see Yamapuri in its full glory from a distance. It shone like a cluster of stars, only even prettier.

This Yamapuri, which normally glistened with all its golden domes and gem-crusted gates, was now looking pale against a very powerful but diminutive light that was blazing forth. This small source of very powerful brilliance came from near the entrance to his house. It completely overshadowed Yamapuri. 'What is that?' wondered Yama.

Dhumorna ran out. Yama jumped off his buffalo and was coming forward with open arms to greet her when Dhumorna stopped him and gestured to her right. And then he saw what she wanted him to see. A young boy, still a child,[5] serious and quiet, was standing close to his house. His brilliance was what Yama had seen even from afar. It had overshadowed the whole of Yamapuri. Pointing to him, Dhumorna urged:

> Entering like fire, is our brahmin guest
> To make him feel welcome, bring water, O Vaivaswata
>
> Hope, expectation, good company, good words,
> Sacrifices and gifts made with piety, sons and cattle
> and all
> Go to waste for the man in whose house
> A brahmin guest stays without taking food.[6]

There was anxiety in her voice. They had a visitor. A little brahmin boy of about ten. His persona was resplendent. And Dhumorna continued with remorse, 'He has been standing in this very posture for three days and three nights. He has refused food or drink. This is no way to treat a guest. And that too such a magnificent-looking one. We have to quickly make amends. I have been waiting for you ever since he came. If we do not satisfy him, you know everything that defines us can go away from us, vanish in this air. All the merit that we have earned with good words, good association, with all the sacrifices and donations we have made … everything will come to naught.

Even what we legitimately hope for as return for all our good deeds will not come to us …'

Yama was not hearing her words any more. His eyes were fixed on that little figure. At one level he was very impressed seeing the child. At another he was full of remorse. A child, and that too such a magnificent-looking brahmin child, had been waiting for him. And the child had refused to partake of any food or drink and was standing as though in penance … waiting for him. Dhumorna was patting him on his arm … Yama came out of his reverie. 'Vaivaswata,' she said in a tone of great urgency, 'go get water to wash the feet of our guest. Attend to him first.'

Yama straightened himself. He was very tall indeed. In a few strides he reached the little figure with a jug of water. The boy was looking straight into space as though lost in his own thoughts.

9
Yama meets Nachiketas

As the sun's rays started escaping out of the horizon, Nachiketas welcomed the new day with hope and expectation. He had seen Yama arrive and looked forward to finally meeting him. Would he have to tell him why he was here or would Yama know, for Yama knew everything about the affairs of men.

Once upon a time there had lived a man called Vajasrava, who performed many yajnas and gave generous gifts in charity. His son was called Vajasravasa, and he was as illustrious as his father. At the moment of speaking, that is just before Nachiketas left to visit Yama, Vajasravasa had been conducting a sacrifice during which he was giving away all that he had in his possession. When performing a special yajna called the Visvajit yajna, it is enjoined that the one who performs it gives away all that he possesses. So that was what Vajasravasa was doing. That yajna was performed specifically for the person doing it to go to heaven.[1] To find a place in heaven. The possessions were given away to the priests who had attended or performed the yajna.

The fire ritual part of the yajna was over and now Vajasravasa was in the process of donating or making gifts to the priests. It was believed that no two people were alike and one had to share one's assets with those who do not have as much as one had oneself.

The gods have not ordained hunger to be the cause
of death, for even a well-fed man dies.
The wealth of the charitable never diminishes, while
the miser finds no comfort in his wealth or society.

He whose kitchen is well stocked but still does not
spare some for the hungry beggar
And instead, with a hard heart, enjoys his meals even
before him will not find comfort either.

Prosperous will be he who feeds the hungry
Attended by success, he will also find friends among
enemies.
He is no friend who does not feed the needy
Better to part ways and seek support of even strangers
We all have two similar hands, but with different
prowess
A cow is unable to feed both her offspring equally
Identical twins may have different strengths and
energies

> Similarly, two brothers differ in the riches they
> possess and donate.[2]

Vajasravasa had a son named Nachiketas. He was still a young boy, a pre-adolescent. Brought up as he was in a household where the grandfather had been inclined to rituals and yajnas, and his father too, Nachiketas seemed to have a natural inclination to keenly observe the actions of his father. He watched his father perform the ritual, taking in every detail. When it came to making the donations, he saw that his father was giving away cattle, no doubt, but they were those that had lived their years. Now they could barely walk. The cows had 'drunk water for the last time, eaten grass for the last time, yielded all their milk and were barren'.[3] In effect, they would be useless anywhere. Their life would soon come to an end.

Nachiketas wondered why his father was giving away what he did not really want. Nobody would want those cattle. Why then palm them off as gifts? Nachiketas seemed to know that when a sacrifice is not performed with the right intent, the desired result is not attained. His father wanted to go to heaven. But he was acting contrary to the instructions given for the yajna, and because of this he could well land up in undesirable places after death. He may not go to the heaven for which he was performing this yajna.

Concerned about his father's welfare, the boy thought, as all children do, that it was up to him to help his father focus on the most important point of the yajna ... the result and not the holding back of property. He went up to his father and asked, 'Father, to whom will you give me?'

Perhaps his father would be forced to reassess what he was doing. Perhaps his father would then talk to him and he, Nachiketas, would be able to point out the mistake he was making in donating his possessions. The father was, however, too busy, as one by one the priests were coming along, accepting gifts, taking them and leaving the premises. What was the point in making these donations, Nachiketas was itching to ask. If it was to go to heaven, then the fact that useless cattle were being donated would considerably reduce the merit that could accrue to his father. Before it got too late, Nachiketas needed to correct him. He was in a hurry. So he asked again, for the second time, 'Father, to whom will you give me?' Again, there was no response from his father.[4]

Nachiketas waited a short while and asked for the third time. Now he was becoming a pest. The father was already a little stressed, perhaps because he knew he was trying to cheat fate. Or perhaps he found his son impertinent. He snapped at his son, 'To Death! To Death I will give you.' It was the equivalent of us saying in the present day, 'Go to hell!'

But a man of the stature of Vajasravasa could not utter loose words. What he spoke happened. Vajasravasa stopped what he was doing. What had he said! Oh, goodness! What had he uttered! Nachiketas too was astounded. His lips parted and his eyes grew round in wonder. Why would his father give him away to Death?

Anyway, the words had been spoken. Nachiketas had to be given to Death. He prepared to meet Yama. Nachiketas reflected that men have come and men have gone … the way corn grows, decays and grows back again. It is a cycle, he thought to himself. The significant aspect of his words at that point was his calling attention to responsibility of conduct among mortals. He said, 'While this cycle of life is continuous, you must remember how your father acted and how others now act.'[5]

Was he trying to draw attention to the impermanence of life and the futility of his father holding back his healthy cows during the yajna? Was he reminding his father of his grandfather's magnanimity and what, therefore, he should follow? Or was he just bidding farewell by saying that dying is no big deal … that it is the way of all men, but what is important is that we be sincere to our purpose while we are still alive, and to that end he recalled his grandfather?

Nachiketas left, for he had been given to Death. That is how he had come here to Yamapuri, where he had been waiting for the past three days. All through these three days, a single thought was trying to find an answer in his head: 'Compared to many, I am among the highest achievers in some matters. I am middling, maybe average, in some other matters. But why would I be then thrown away to Death? Am I so unworthy of life? And, further, what would Death gain through me?'[6]

He had received some education, so he knew what yajnas were meant for and how they should be performed. He was sincere and conscientious. He did not lack in self-esteem. He did not think, 'I must be like those cows, useless, and so my father is giving me away.' He made a true assessment of himself. Now the question he needed to find an answer to was what Death would achieve through him. He also needed to experience the place his father sought to reach after death.

At that point Nachiketas saw Yama standing before him in all humility. Yama said:

> Three nights have you dwelt in this house of mine
> Without taking a morsel, O honoured guest.
> I prostrate before you O brahmin, may good befall me
> And to make amends, three boons I grant to you,
> to pick.[7]

The little boy had Yama appealing to him for his blessings. It is true that the guest was not to be neglected, and the belief that the unhappy guest could curse was very strong. But more than that, Yama was touched by a visitor coming to him of his own accord. Having come, he was not distracted by Yama's beautiful city, which would definitely have tried to lure the youngster in many ways. He had a purpose. Yama was also amused. To make it easier for the guest to accomplish his purpose, he had granted him the boons. As for the remorse he felt for not hosting his guest properly, it was genuine. Yama himself does not relent when someone makes a mistake. His accountant Chitragupta records it instantly. Yama was unforgiving about his own remiss, and so he prayed to Nachiketas that he should not be punished for this neglect. May good befall me, he requested the boy.

Little Nachiketas did not have to think so much, like Yama. He had his answer ready.

> Pacified and kindly, let my father be towards me
> As before. By you, when I am sent back
> He should know and greet me too
> This is the first of the three boons I ask, O Death![8]

Yama smiled. This was going to be easy. The little child wanted his father to be happy with him. Every child yearns for approval from his father. Had he been talking to his daughter, Sunita,[9] when she was a child, he would have picked her up and placed her on his lap. But now he was being formal. This child also stood his ground, a young but mature seeker. Yama was also amused because Nachiketas was sure he was only a visitor, he was sure Yama would send him back. That is confidence, thought Yama.

So he led Nachiketas into his house. The sun had come up and the gems embedded on the facade of his house were flashing its reflection. It was not comfortable to stand there any longer. Into the mansion, which was 200 yojanas in length and 50 yojanas in height, Yama walked, along with Nachiketas. Golden doors were opened and innumerable pillars embedded with emeralds glistened. Yama and Nachiketas walked up crystal staircases. The walls were decorated with diamonds. Yama led his guest into his assembly hall. As he observed him from the corner of his eye, he found that Nachiketas did not look around at his palace in awe or wonder. The best of kings and sages had gasped in amazement on entering his palace. In fact, the grandeur of Yama's palace had left them speechless. But Nachiketas was walking as fast as his little legs could carry him and remained untouched by all that surrounded him.

Yama led Nachiketas to the assembly hall, which was huge, well lit and cheerful. It was neither hot nor cold inside. Here Yama sat his guest on a seat and himself sat facing him. Gentle strains of music from a flute wafted in.

Yama leaned forward and answered Nachiketas:

Due to my favour, when you go back
He[10] will be to you as he was before
After sleeping well, will become free from anger
On seeing you return from the jaws of Death[11]

Nachiketas was happy, but looked ready to seek his next boon.

10

Yama grants Nachiketas his second boon

Happy to see Nachiketas reassured that his father would no longer be angry with him, Yama smiled encouragingly at the young boy. Nachiketas cleared his throat softly and began the request for his second boon:

In heaven, there is no fear
You are not there, nor is there fear of old age
Having gone beyond hunger, thirst and sorrow
One rejoices in heaven.

O Death! You know the altar wherein the fire created
Leads to that heaven, the dwellers of which enjoy
immortality
I am full of faith, and request you to recollect that and
Explain that to me as my second boon.[1]

Yama wanted to laugh out aloud! This little boy who did not even reach up to his knees in height was telling him to his face that he wanted to know the secret to get to that heaven because he, Yama, was not there! Yama was indeed the most feared king! But he did not laugh as he was afraid his guest would get offended. The boy had some gall, he thought.

His face turned grave as he reflected on the question. It was a selfless boon to ask for. Yama thought the boy, after asking for the well-being of his father, would ask for more material boons to make his life on earth more comfortable. But now he was asking about the heaven to go to which his father had been performing the special yajna. He now wanted to ensure the next step for his father, the heaven after death. Yama was impressed with the young boy.

Dhumorna, who was passing that way, could not help a smile when she heard Nachiketas's question. She was happy the little guest was being taken care of and that her husband had granted him boons. She was also happy with the question Nachiketas was asking because she knew Yama loved to speak about Agni, or fire, so closely did Yama identify Agni with himself. 'Agni is the leader of the sacrifice and protects it in the great journey against the powers of darkness. The knowledge and purpose of this divine Puissance can be entirely trusted; he is the friend and lover of the soul and will not betray it to evil gods.'[2]

The magnificence of Agni comes from the fact that even though it can move in every direction, the force of its primary movement is always upward. That is why Agni is worshipped as a link between this world and the world of gods. This fire is not one that comes with striking a match, it is one that has been kindled ritualistically.

Yama wanted to tell Nachiketas a story about Agni. But Nachiketas was looking far too intently at him, waiting to have the route map to that heaven where there was no Yama and no fear of old age, hunger or sorrow. When Nachiketas said so surely, 'You are not there,' Yama did not want to correct him. Yama was everywhere. In the highest heaven were people who had accumulated a lot of good karmas. If they attained enlightenment in the meanwhile, it would be great for them and they would not be born on earth. Otherwise they would be brought back to earth to live a mortal life all over again. In the other heavens too there was an end time, an expiry date. As soon as one's stock of good karmas was over, the being would be transported back to earth.[3]

But Yama did not bother to tell Nachiketas the story of Agni because that was not the point that Nachiketas was seeking clarification on. Nachiketas was sincerely asking a question, reposing intense faith in the answer that Yama would give on how mankind could use that fire ritual to redeem itself after death.

Yama now taught the eager Nachiketas:

To you I will tell, and you learn from me
About that fire altar which leads to heaven,

O Nachiketas of fine understanding
That great fire which leads to heaven and supports
the earth
Lies hidden in the cavity of the heart.[4]

Yama explained the ritual step by step. He told him of the greatness of Agni and how Agni was the source of the universe and its support. He spoke in detail about the construction of the altar, the number of bricks to be used and their placement. Having finished teaching Nachiketas about the ritual and the right procedure for it, he asked the boy if he had understood what he had explained. Nachiketas repeated verbatim everything that Yama had said. Yama was touched and delighted. He said:

I grant to you another extra boon
Henceforth this ritual will be known by your name,
the Nachiketas Fire Sacrifice
And do accept this gift[5] too.[6]

Yama went on to elaborate the qualifications of the one who sets out to perform the yajna, the number of times it should be performed in one's lifetime and the benefits that would accrue to the performer of the Nachiketas yajna. The one who performed the yajna satisfactorily would be able to go the highest heaven where there is no sorrow (and no Yama as per Nachiketas).[7] Yama finished his answer by saying:

This, Nachiketas, is the fire that leads to heaven
Which you sought from me as your second boon
This fire will be spoken of by people by your name
only
Now O Nachiketas, ask your third boon.[8]

There were many eavesdroppers trying to catch the conversation between Nachiketas and Yama. 'What did Yama teach Nachiketas? What did Nachiketas reply?' they asked each other. Somehow they seemed to have missed it all! Yama knew. Now Nachiketas knew. No one else did.

Yama thought Nachiketas would be pleased to hear the fire ritual was now named after him. He smiled patronisingly at Nachiketas, waiting for him to speak.

11

Nachiketas asks for his third boon

Nachiketas was ready. He did not seem flattered that Yama had made his name immortal by naming an important ritual after him. Nachiketas was focused on what he was going to ask next. He had now ensured that his father would be nice to him. He had also learned what to tell his father and others who wanted to go to heaven about the yajna they had to perform. The request which followed was finally for himself:

> There is some confusion about a person, dead
> Some say he exists, some say he does not.
> I want clarification through instruction from you
> This is what I seek for my third boon.[1]

Yama was stumped. What a question! Nachiketas was asking what happens after death. Do you still live, or do you not? Yama replied easily to Nachiketas:

Even the gods have wondered about this, long, long
ago
It is not easy to comprehend, for the answer is too
subtle in nature.
Ask for another boon, Nachiketas
Please do not persist with this, release me from it.[2]

Yama was ready to dismiss the boy's request. He turned his attention from Nachiketas and looked out, far away. Nachiketas observed Yama's reluctance to grant him the boon he had asked for. He spoke thus:

Oh! If even the gods have debated upon this
Then it must indeed be difficult to understand, as
you have just said.
Where then will I find another teacher like you?
There can be none other.
And so there can be no boon equal to this one.[3]

Yama felt cornered. At one level he felt he must answer this little boy who was so eager, so genuine. At another level it was going to be a challenge. How was he to answer this child?

Nachiketas was looking at him earnestly. Yama leaned forward and told the boy gently, in a voice that was sweet and soft:

> Ask for sons and grandsons who will live to be centenarians
> Ask for plenty of livestock, elephants and horses, even gold
> Ask for a wide expanse of the earth as belonging to you
> Ask for as many years to live as you would wish for yourself.[4]

Such riches he was willing to bestow on Nachiketas. 'Ask,' said Yama, 'for things that are tangible.' And then he added, thinking he may have missed something a youngster would yearn for:

> Nachiketas! If you think there is any other boon
> That equals or surpasses wealth with longevity
> And vast lands in your possession, then ask of me
> I will gladly ensure you enjoy it all, Nachiketas.[5]

Yama smiled at Nachiketas, trying to add to the lure of his words. No one could refuse all this, thought Yama. Of course, to say no one would be too much of a generalisation. There was Garuda, born of Vinata, who chose knowledge over worldly temptations.

Vinata and Kadru were wives of the Rishi Kashyapa. Rishi Kashyapa gave each of his wives a boon. Kadru wished to have a thousand snakes for sons. Vinata asked for just two sons, stronger than the thousand sons of Kadru.

Kadru gave birth to a thousand eggs after many long years. Five hundred years later the eggs hatched and the snakes came wriggling out. Vinata was now restless. Her two eggs had not hatched. She paced up and down restlessly till, unable to resist the temptation, she broke one egg open. Out of that emerged Aruna, who became Yama's father Surya's charioteer. He chastened Vinata and told her not to disturb the other egg.

In the meanwhile, Kadru managed to win a wager with Vinata, as a result of which Vinata became her slave. When Garuda emerged, cracking his egg, his mother was not around. She was in the service of Kadru. Garuda was very upset that his mother was enslaved. He asked the thousand sons of Kadru what they would take as a price to release his mother from bondage. 'Amrita!' they all screamed in unison. The ocean had been churned and the gods were in possession of the ambrosia that had been got from the churning. Garuda spread his large wings and flew heavenwards. He picked up the jar of nectar, though it was well guarded, and was flying down when Indra met him. 'Allow me to place the jar on the ground near the snakes and get release for my mother. No sooner do I place it than you may take the jar back to heaven,' Garuda told Indra. Indra agreed. And that is what happened.

Yama recollected that story because when Vishnu saw Garuda, he found that Garuda was not interested in taking a little of the elixir for himself. Vishnu made him his vehicle in appreciation of this and also carried a flag with the emblem of Garuda, thus extolling the rectitude of the great bird. It was Garuda who had sought knowledge from Vishnu himself, and one conversation of theirs became known as *Garuda Purana*. Garuda became immortal even without partaking of the elixir. But then, Garuda was born of the will and austerity of great rishis. These rishis had wanted to create another Indra but had been persuaded not to disturb the existing set-up. Garuda was thus born of the power of penance.[6]

Nachiketas may yield, thought Yama. He added nevertheless:

> Whatever you desire, however rare they be
> Ask, Nachiketas, ask to your heart's desire, ask for
> them all.
> Here, look at these beautiful maidens on the chariots
> They play musical instruments too
> Their kind cannot be found on earth, enjoy them
> Nachiketas
> I will give them to you, they will serve you
> But, about death, do not question me.[7]

As he spoke he wondered if anyone had heard him offering Nachiketas all this. They would consider him such a fraud! He spent all his time telling people not to be lured by the temptations of the material world. And here he was himself offering them to Nachiketas. A pre-adolescent boy. He was leading him beyond his years with ideas of women and wealth. But he had his reasons for this. Though he had said what he did, what he still abided by was his standard guidelines to mortals:

Wealth is like a pleasant dream, youth can be
compared to a flower
Life is fleeting as lightning, where does the
discerning find peace?[8]

He who has no discernment
Imagines benefit in the harmful
Views the impermanent as permanent and
Thinks that which is evil is good[9]

Sleep, lust, hunger, are to all living beings the same
The one with knowledge is called a man; the other
beast
A man is the knowledgeable, discerning one; the
other is a beast.[10]

Nachiketas had heard his many offers. If the boy chose any of them, the matter would end. Yama would send him back safely to earth. Yama would also know he was not a worthy student. That was why Yama was speaking so to Nachiketas, offering him all the temptations of the material world. It was important to know if the student was adequately serious to receive the knowledge he was asking for, which could not be shared with the unworthy.

Now it was Nachiketas's turn to smile. In the presence of Death, also called Antaka or Mrtyu, the one who takes you away from all the good and bad of this world, how could Nachiketas's mind dwell on the pleasures that Yama was offering him? That was the first time the enormity of death was articulated by Nachiketas. Helpless are those who stand in front of death – would they be lured by any material pleasures? He knew they would be short-lived because Yama would come to take him away sooner or later. The question remained: what happens then, what happens after death?

O Death, transient are these sensual pleasures of the mortal man
They just consume the vigour of inner fire of the being
And what to say of the longest life which is still too short
Keep for yourself, O Death, all your vehicles, dances and songs.

To what end will wealth serve
Particularly after meeting you?
We live as long as you wish it
And so this boon alone is what I seek of you.

Having had just a whiff of the ageless and immortal,
Which mortal with discernment,
Ageing as he is in the world below, still seek to
Derive pleasures from a long life, beauty or love?

The point where humanity turns blank
That you must explain to me
What happens when we pass beyond
Tell me, O Death, let me into this secret
Other than which Nachiketas wishes nothing else.[11]

Yama took a deep breath. At one level he felt he must tell this little boy the secret. He was so sincere, so keen to know. At another level, it was going to be a challenge. How was he to answer this child? He should be able to teach well and his student should be able to grasp well. The prayer that automatically moved Yama's lips was:

Om! May God protect the teacher and the taught
May we grow together in knowledge

May we together reap the results of our effort
May we truly excel in our studies
May disagreements not divide us
Om shanti shanti shanti.[12]

12

Yama tests the student

Having firmly refused all that Yama was trying to tempt him with, and having also articulated clearly why, Nachiketas looked at Yama to see how he was reacting. What more temptations could Yama place before him? Nachiketas, however, saw a calm and serious face. He saw a teacher – so unmistakably that he automatically brought his palms together in reverence for the teaching he was about to receive.

Yama now looked at Nachiketas as a teacher would a good student. His eyes grew moist looking at such a rare find – a good and receptive student.

Yama's memory stretched back in time to remember the story of Sudarsana, his friend Agni's son. Sudarsana married a beautiful and virtuous woman, Oghavati. He resolved to conquer death. But friend or foe, Yama had to keep his dharma. He could not let Sudarsana take such a resolve and simply sit and watch. So Yama started to stalk him to catch him when he slipped up. He walked by him as Death; he watched over him as Dharma.[1]

Sudarsana had taken a vow: to be as hospitable as possible to any guest who visited, to never reject any of their requests, never leave anything undone for them. He instructed Oghavati too accordingly, and she promised to follow his instructions for the benefit of her husband. 'Even if it means giving up your life, honour your guest's requests,' he told her. The idea behind this was that nothing belonged to him. He was a guest himself on earth.

One day, when Sudarsana had gone to the forest to collect firewood, a brahmin came visiting Oghavati. She was hospitable and served him with care. 'I want your personal favour,' said the brahmin. 'I just want your person.' Oghavati was repulsed, but the promise she had made to her husband resounded in her ears. She tried to satisfy the brahmin by making every other possible offering. But he was insistent. Finally, steeling herself, she gave in.

Soon enough, Sudarsana returned home. He knocked on the door. There was silence from within. How was Oghavati to tell her husband that a brahmin guest was all set to take advantage of her? Her voice froze. There was another knock. The brahmin spoke, 'Sudarsana, as you had instructed your wife, she was hospitable to me, and my only desire was for her and now she is giving herself to me.'

Sudarsana's head and back straightened just a little bit. Death was ready to strike. Sudarsana would surely lose his composure now. But Sudarsana said, 'To please a guest is our privilege.' He added, 'Nothing belongs to me. O foremost of virtuous men, the five elements, fire, water, earth, air and sky, and the mind, the intellect and the soul, time and space and the ten organs of sense are all present in the bodies of men and always witness the good and evil deeds that men do. This truth has been uttered by me today and let the gods bless me for it or destroy me if I have spoken falsely.'

The brahmin immediately came out of the house and revealed himself as Dharma, none other than Death himself. Praising Sudarsana, he said, 'This was but a test in which you and your truthful wife have emerged faultless and worthy of praise. Your wife is too righteous a lady to be harmed. The whole world salutes her. And you have truly conquered Mrtyu, for you have all your senses and emotions under control. Sudarsana, you will go with your body to heaven, while Oghavati will go half with you, and her other half will flow as a river on earth.'

Yama had met in Sudarsana a man who had chosen the path of shreyas, conquering all the elements, the mind, time, space, as also desire and anger. Now he was sitting with a ten-year-old who had refused all his offers of the best possible riches in the world. Nachiketas was also choosing the path of shreyas, as had Garuda and Sudarsana.

This was also why Yama was very repentant about his guest Nachiketas having been left waiting for him for three days and nights without food or water. As Dharma, the brahmin had presented an extreme provocation to Sudarsana to lose his temper and show his desire for possessions. Sudarsana had not fallen for the bait. Here too Yama had presented to Nachiketas all kinds of temptations, and Nachiketas had not fallen for the bait either.

Yama cleared his throat and began to describe the right student to whom this knowledge could be imparted. The teaching had commenced.

'There are two paths,' said Yama, 'that of shreyas and that of preyas.[2] They are different from each other. Shreyas is the beneficial path while preyas is the path that appears pleasant, and so attractive. The beneficial path may or may not be pleasant. Both these paths create bondages. Good befalls him who chooses the path of shreyas, while the one who chooses preyas loses his way in his journey to the ultimate goal. A human being is faced with the choice of both paths: shreyas and preyas. They lie parallel to each other and can never be one. The discerning one chooses the former while the materially inclined choose the latter.'

> One is beneficial while the other attractive
> Though leading towards divergent goals,
> They both bind human beings. Of the two,
> The one who chooses the good is blessed
> The other loses his way to the true end.
>
> All humans are faced with the choice of
> The beneficial and the attractive paths
> The discerning, after consideration, chooses the beneficial
> The dullard, due to avarice and attachment, chooses the attractive.[3]

And then Yama told his student:

> And you? Lovable and beautiful objects of desire
> Assessing them rightly, you have renounced, O Nachiketas
> You have not chosen the path of material riches
> The quagmire within which many have lost themselves.[4]

The teacher proceeded to commend his student further, and in the following verse concluded what he had been trying to say in the earlier three:

> Divergent and distant are the two, leading as they do
>   to different ends,
> That which is known as knowledge and that which is
>   known as ignorance.
> Desirous of knowledge is Nachiketas
> Not in the least tempted by desires.
>
> Those who live in the cocoon of ignorance
> Consider themselves wise and discerning people
> These ignoramuses are going round in circles of
>   delusion
> Indeed, the blind leading the blind, as it were.
>
> To the immature, the world hereafter is not apparent
> Wealth throws the ignorant into a stupor
> So much so that he thinks there is nothing beyond
> And so keeps coming back to me for dispensation.[5]

The state of the ignorant reminded him of the hunter Arjunaka. Yama had once met an old woman called Gautami who had one day found her son dead from a snakebite. A hunter by the name of Arujnaka found the snake who had bitten the boy. Grabbing it and tying it with a string, he brought it to Gautami and said, 'Look, I have found the wretch that killed your son. How do you want me to kill it?'

Gautami was of a calm and realised nature. 'However you kill it, it will not give my son back to me, so let it be,' she replied.

The hunter was appalled. Thinking he was bringing justice to the world, he said, 'You do not talk like one who has experienced grief. This snake will go on to bite many others … we must kill it. Shall I chop it into bits or shall I throw it into a blazing fire?'

This interaction went on for some time, with Gautami maintaining her stance and Arjunaka remaining just as indignant and angry. He wanted to ensure justice and thought it could be done by killing the one who had caused the boy's death.

Then the snake finally spoke up to clarify the matter. 'It is not my fault,' said the snake. 'Mrtyu sent me, and so I did his bidding.'

More discussion ensued. Finally, Mrtyu himself appeared. 'I am not at fault, nor is the serpent. It is the fault of Kala, or Time,' said Mrtyu.

'The serpent and Mrtyu are the cause of the boy's death,' Arunjaka maintained. 'I wish to avenge the boy's death.'

The serpent said the matter had to be considered more thoroughly. Arjunaka asked, 'If you both, serpent and Mrtyu, are dependent on Kala, I wish to know how Kala becomes a cause.'

Mrtyu explained that everything – the act of doing good or evil – is caused and recorded by Kala. Kala decides. Being discussed so much caused Kala also to appear. 'The acts that one performs catches up with the person in time. That is called karma. This boy died because of his karma. Both good actions and evil actions bind us in karma. People suffer according to their actions. Therefore, choose the beneficial path so that one day you will be relieved from this cycle of birth and death,' said Kala.

So Yama recollected how he had to present himself as both Death and Time to convince the hunter that the path of preyas brings people back to him repeatedly in a cycle of birth and death.

Yama had now told Nachiketas that both shreyas and preyas bind man. To the man who follows the path that is attractive, the world hereafter is not apparent. To avenge the boy's death, the killing of the serpent may bring some calm to the hunter's mind. But that would only be more negative action and would have bound him in evil karma, bringing him back to Yama's court. A person like Gautami knew the path of shreyas and so kept her calm.[6]

Yama told Nachiketas:

Even to hear of this great Truth, many do not get a
chance
Many of those who do still do not comprehend
Rare is the teacher who knows the Self
Even rarer is the one who learns from him.[7]

13

Yama reveals the Truth

Yama felt a lot of affection for Nachiketas. At one level he felt happy, as all teachers do when they find a sincere and earnest student. At another level his appreciation for Nachiketas was very personal: it was an appreciation of the qualities that this little boy was exhibiting, against which Yama felt even the most evolved sages compared poorly.

The knowledge Nachiketas was seeking was very complex. Therefore it was important for the seeker to exercise caution when choosing the teacher from whom this knowledge was to be learned, and equally for the teacher in selecting the right student to learn it. Yama had already described the qualities of a student. He now began to describe the teacher.

Being realised, Yama could see the past, present and future. In fact, Yama was called Kala because he himself was Time. As we have seen, Time was born of Yama. He had seen many times that the Ultimate was sought to be explained by the realised. But being extremely subtle, it was neither easy to comprehend nor easy to describe for comprehension. He could see how Narayana Himself would instruct his (Yama's) son Yudhishthira[1] in the future.

Yama could clearly see what Narayana, incarnated as Krishna, would tell Yudhishthira to bring his focus back to the path of spirituality.[2] Much of what Yama had told Nachiketas and some of what he was going to tell him now would be beautifully explained by Narayana. He, Narayana, would explain it all using the most distinguishing feature of the human mind: its insatiable capacity for desire. Krishna would even quote the words of Kama, or Desire. Kama was indestructible, unless the practitioner could focus on Brahman alone. That was the only way to destroy desire. If man instead chose prayer to destroy Kama, Kama would use the same technique to create more aspirations in that person as to what could be wrought through prayer. This was also true if a practitioner chose to make sacrifices: Kama would ensure he would have desires as to what he would gain from the sacrifices. These rituals are called sakama, or sacrifices performed with desire. So desire is the most difficult impulse to conquer. If a man owning half the earth is not attached to his wealth, has no feeling of possession, he is ready for salvation, as Sudarsana had so effectively shown. But if a man sitting in the forest, wearing the bark of a tree and carrying a rosary, is still possessive about his material assets even in his penance, he has not progressed at all. He will have to repeatedly go through cycles of birth and death. So Narayana, incarnated as Krishna, told Yudhishthira that Mrtyu is a two-syllable word, under the sway of which people like the seeming ascetic in the forest come. This means that the ascetic, even though performing great penance, will not be saved from mortality since he is only pretending. People like him have a lot of the sense of 'mine-ness' towards the material world. Shasvat is a three-syllable word, meaning the eternal, or Brahman. It cannot be accessed by giving up external paraphernalia. In people who want to access eternity, the sense of 'mine-ness' is absent. An example of this is Sudarsana. So the giving up comes from within, since these two, Brahman and Mrtyu, have their seats in the souls of all creatures. But they remain unseen.

'Therefore, wise men, knowing this, subjugate their desires. The yogi who holds communion with the Supreme Spirit knows yoga[3] to be the perfect way (to salvation) by reason of the practices done in his many former births. And remembering that what the soul desires is not conducive to piety and virtue, and that suppression of the desires is at the root of all true virtue, such men do not engage in the practice of charity, Vedic learning, asceticism and Vedic rites whose object is attainment of worldly prosperity, ceremonies, sacrifices, religious rules and meditation with the motive of securing any advantage thereby.'[4]

It was desire that Nachiketas had rejected in every form that desire could present itself. Not even an adolescent yet, this boy had shown the maturity of saying he was not interested in securing any advantage for himself. He just wanted to know That, knowing which everything else becomes known.

To complete the story about Yudhishthira … he had been despondent. As the eldest of the Pandavas, he had won the Mahabharata war and returned to Hastinapura, but he was feeling very sorrowful because so many of his family members had died. That was when Krishna told him about Shasvat, the eternal. Krishna was motivating Yudhishthira to perform the Ashvamedha yajna, or horse sacrifice. Yudhishthira said the war had emptied the coffers of his kingdom. Krishna motivated Yudhishthira to mine for wealth, saying that there was no use of grieving for the people lost. They were gone, but only in physical form, as the soul is indestructible and eternal. Krishna also told him that people like the ones who had gone would repeatedly come under the sway of Mrtyu. 'So direct your desires towards making large donations and sacrifices, at least you will benefit from it.'

Yama thought of this incident not only because it was about his son's personal experience but also because it described just the kind of person he was going to tell Nachiketas about. Remember the example of the sage in the forest wearing the bark of a tree, carrying a rosary and living on fruits but still possessive and materially inclined? If such a person were to teach the truth about the Self, Yama cautioned Nachiketas, it would lead to nowhere. A material perspective cannot lead to spiritual insight. The teacher needed to have taken that leap of faith and overcome material attachments. The teacher needed to have known Brahman – to be one who holds no difference between himself and the Supreme.

A person of inferior mental attitudes cannot teach about the Self
For it is difficult to understand that which is known variously
And there is no way to know it unless taught
And is knowable only from that person who is one with It (Brahman)
For the Self is subtler than the subtlest, unobtainable through mere reason

Unobtainable by argumentation
Yet easy to understand when taught
By the teacher who holds no biases

To one who is steadfast and perseverant like you
May there be more such, O Nachiketas
Who can enquire so.[5]

Elaborating, and once again touching on his own personal journey, Yama continued:

I know the treasures gained by the fruits of action
 are transient
The eternal is not to be reached by the non-eternal
Therefore, I built the Nachiketas fire altar
And by things non-eternal have gained the eternal.[6]

Yama's journey to this heaven had been the first. Ever since, he had tried to prepare different methods that could be followed by those aspiring to be in his heaven. Performance of the fire sacrifice, which he taught Nachiketas and had since named it after the boy, was one of them. But Nachiketas did not have to go through all that. He did not have to perform yajnas and sacrifices, make donations and do acts of charity, because he knew they were all born of desire, even though it might be better than material pursuit. They were born of the desire to ensure oneself better life after death and to seek the benevolence of the Supreme so that one is saved from fear.

The world which is founded on the fulfilment of
desire
The rewards that accrue with continuous
performance of sacrifices
Helping one cross over to the shore of fearlessness
Great and praiseworthy is the destination[7] of such
penance
All of which you have considered and rejected,
O Nachiketas.[8]

The highest of heavens that one can reach after performing all the rituals is a place where all desires are fulfilled, where there is no fear, where one can get the highest satisfaction and happiness, and even that Nachiketas had rejected because all that still did not tell him what made the world tick. His question was as simple as that.

Yama finally introduced to Nachiketas that Brahman:

Difficult to experience, hidden in the cave of the
heart within
Inaccessible and inscrutable is the ancient one
dwelling therein
By means of meditation on the Self one recognises
the Lord within
And thereupon, joys and sorrows renounces.

Yama told Nachiketas that in every person's heart, in its deep recesses, lives the Brahman, the Supreme, the Self, the Atman. It is difficult to reach it as it is covered by layers and layers of the experiences of our senses and the mesh of ignorance. It is inscrutable because it cannot be seen, and so inferences cannot be drawn about it. It has to be experienced. Once experienced, the experiencer becomes one with Brahman, or the One and Only.

> This, having heard, understanding it well, the mortal
> Extracts the virtuous, the righteous and subtle Atman
> Veiled by ignorance,
> And rejoices in this attainment of that which is the cause of this joy
> This house of Brahman is open to Nachiketas, I believe.[9]

As he added to his great revelation, Yama tilted his head in question. Nachiketas was stilled by the Truth he had just experienced from Yama's exposition. He just stared at Yama with a faraway look in his eyes. And thus Yama taught Nachiketas the greatest Truth …

14

This indeed is That, said Yama

And thus Yama grandly threw open the doors to the Ultimate for Nachiketas. Nachiketas was now not just fit to experience Brahman, he was also adequately empowered to experience Brahman. The excitement was infectious when Nachiketas said:

> Tell me about That which you see
> As other than right and other than wrong
> As neither the cause nor the effect
> As other than the past and other than the future.

Tell me about That, tell me, urged Nachiketas. Despite having so much wisdom and tenacity of purpose, and a lofty purpose at that, Nachiketas had always been a little impatient. He had pestered his father, as a result of which he had been impulsively cursed to go to Death. Now he could not wait for Yama to give him everything, every little bit of detail. Yama smiled. He understood this restlessness. This was one of the vital qualifications for a seeker ... he needed to be obsessed about attaining Brahman. Nachiketas was just that. From asking what happens after death, he had now understood enough to ask to be described That which his teacher seemed to know so well. Nachiketas too wanted to be one with That. He wanted more teaching, and urgently.

Once again Yama was impressed with the little boy. He had asked a true Vedantic question now. Earlier, he had repeated verbatim the details of the Nachiketas fire sacrifice that Yama had taught him. Now, having understood his description of Brahman, the boy wanted to know more. Sensing the urgency being experienced by Nachiketas, Yama decided to give him the short cut to Brahman. He said:

> The word that all the Vedas celebrate
> The word that all penances proclaim
> Desiring which the life of a brahmachary[1] is followed
> That word I will now tell you in brief
> It is Om.
>
> This word alone is Brahman
> This word alone is Supreme
> By knowing this word alone
> One gets everything that one desires.

The word is a support beyond compare
It is the support supreme
By knowing this support
One rejoices in Brahmaloka.

The wise one (the Self) is
Neither born nor dies
It does not come from anywhere nor does anything
come from it
It is eternal, undecaying and ancient
It is not destroyed when the body is.[2]

Yama had already told Nachiketas that the Self is hidden in the secret cave of each human being's heart. So Yama had told him the greatest secret – and what has come to be called the Mahavakya ... *Etadvai tat*, or This is indeed That.[3]

The secret was out.

A quiet filled the air. Nachiketas was taking a deep breath in. Yama spoke again after what seemed an eternal pause. His tone was soft, his voice smooth, like flowing butter. The moment was all that was, neither a past nor a present engulfed it. In that moment, Yama elaborated on the secret part by part. He first spoke of the subtle Self, which has been described as the tension of opposites ... it combines both ends of any scale and therefore rises above it, like a triangle. The opposites form the two basal points of the triangle. Truth is neither held down by this point or the other … it rises above both to encompass both and yet is different, as it is way above them. It is so subtle that if a being thinks he is destroyed, as in killed, or is destroying, in neither case does he know that It – the Self or Atman or Brahman – cannot be killed or kill. It is eternal. It never dies. Furthermore, It does not get sullied by day-to-day actions. It is beyond that. Yama explained that when we say It is both joyful and joyless, it means It neither withers with bad news nor blooms with good news. This does not mean that the person does not experience or respond to joy and sorrow. He or she does, but deep within there is no change.

It is hard to understand, said Yama, because of the limitations of the human mind. The human mind is able to imagine primarily within the parameters of the known. That is why once, when Rishi Markandeya was meditating and Yama visited him, the sage asked, 'How can one repay one's debts to one's parents? How can one attain the eternal glorious world, so difficult to attain?'

Markandeya was asking how one could attain the heavens. In his reply Yama was eloquent about how one must follow one's dharma, which is something the mind can comprehend. And that would eventually, with continual practice, bring equanimity. Yama gives him instructions to reach the heavens in terms of easily comprehensible steps. He says:

> Penance, purity, to be devoted to truth and dharma
> all the time
> Worship of parents are mandatory
> Many Ashvamedha sacrifices and generous gifts
> Then to the extraordinary world of Brahman, the
> practitioner will attain.[4]

Now it may be easier to understand why Krishna advised Yudhishthira to perform the horse sacrifice after the war.

Many people would be able to understand up to this step and therefore try to follow these instructions. This is the ritualistic part of the story. Yama's advice to Markandeya was given to help keep the mind under control. To keep the mind under control is vital if one wants to reach heaven. To realise Brahman, which is what Nachiketas wanted, went far beyond even that. It was a different game altogether, and that was the great secret that Yama unlocked for Nachiketas.

What did Yama tell Nachiketas? He told Nachiketas that the short cut to get to Brahman is Om.

> This word alone is Brahman
> This word alone is Supreme

By knowing this word alone
One gets everything that one desires.

Yama continued to describe Brahman, though It defies description. In a sentence, which in later times came to be often quoted, Yama said, 'It is very subtle, subtler than the subtlest, greater than the greatest; It is stationary and yet moving far distances.' In this brief but elegant way, Yama told Nachiketas, 'And It is all-pervading and so does not have to move to be everywhere. It is sleeping and yet travelling. It is both joyful and joyless and located in the heart of every being. A person whose mind is not clouded with attachment will be able to perceive the Self, for then the mind is pure. When it is not bound by the strings of attachment, the mind too becomes limitless. This Atman, which has no body, sits in perishable bodies, and cannot be attained through study, sermons or intelligence, nor in full measure by simply hearing about It. It is attained only by one who chooses to attain It. And to him the Atman reveals Its true nature.'

The act of choosing to attain Brahman is not as simple as choosing between one piece of apparel and another. It means following the path of righteousness through and through. The one who does not do that, the one whose senses are not subdued, whose mind does not have clarity of purpose, cannot attain the Self through knowledge. Knowledge is assumed if one has the ability to choose the right path. Those who opt for the pleasures of the senses and live in their attachments are the ignorant ones. Such people, notwithstanding the social position they may hold, live only to feed Death.

Using the metaphor of the chariot, Yama elaborated:

Look at that Atman as the lord of the chariot
Of the body as the chariot
The intellect as the charioteer
And the mind as the reins

Driving the chariot are the horses, likened to the senses
The routes they tread upon are the sense objects
The discriminating ones say that linked to the body and mind
The Self is bhokta or the one who enjoys these pleasures

A person lacking the right understanding
Is always of an uncontrolled, unrestrained mind
His senses too act in that unrestrained manner
As a rebellious horse towards his charioteer

One who has the right understanding
Always sports a calm, restrained mind

Then the senses fall in line
As a well-trained, obedient horse with their
charioteer[5]

The first kind of person, whose mind is not in control, loses his way to enlightenment. He gets caught in the cycle of birth and death. The second kind reaches Vishnu Himself. Yama now added words of caution – do not go by your intellect alone, Brahman lies even beyond that. To improve Nachiketas's understanding, Yama gives him a visual picture:

The sense objects are higher than the senses
The mind is higher than the sense objects
The intellect is higher than the mind
And the expansive Soul is higher than the intellect

The unmanifest is higher than the expansiove soul
The purusha (person) is higher that the unmanifest
And higher than the purusha, there is nothing at all
That is the end, He is the goal

Hidden as He is in every being
Invisible he is for appearances
The wise ones who can see the subtle
Spot Him with their refined focus and fine
perception[6]

The motivating teacher goes on to tell Nachiketas that though the path is tough and uncompromising, the result is beautiful. Where does it lead to? To within the human being. And Yama then put it poetically:

The wise should draw into the mind their words of
speech
Draw the mind into the intellect
Draw the intellect into the Atman
And rest with the Atman in the peaceful Self[7]

Describing thus the power of restraint as the key instrument with which to realise Brahman or Atman, Yama exhorted his disciple to:

Arise, awake
Having obtained what you wanted
Like the razor's edge, is the path to cross
Sharp and difficult, say the wise poets

It is without sound, without touch, without form,
without decay
Without taste, without smell, eternal, without
beginning, without end
Perceiving, the great and unchanging
One goes beyond the grasp of death[8]

Yama ended his lesson with a benedictory line for all those who would in time hear of his conversation with Nachiketas. He said the intelligent one who tells the story of Nachiketas as told by him, Yama, will be glorified in the world of Brahman. And the one who tells the story at a gathering, to an assembly of people or at the time when a soul is departing will gain immortality.[9]

Book 5

THE INDULGENT BENEFACTOR

15

Yama leaves Yamapuri

Yama saw him from a distance. There was an urgency in his manner and a quickness in his step. Yama knew why he was hurrying to come and meet him. He smiled to himself.

'Chitragupta!' he called out, when the man was close. 'I know why you are coming. I remember what I have to do today, don't worry.' Chitragupta was Yama's minister who recorded the good and evil done by men. He slowed his pace slightly. But he looked like he still had something to say. Before he could come closer, offer his respects to his master, Lord of Death, and say what he wished to, Yama spoke again: 'I have decided to go myself.' Chitragupta shook his head ever so slightly. It was clear he did not approve, but he could not tell his master that. 'You have able-bodied messengers … send them … why trouble yourself?' he suggested.

Yama laughed. He understood his minister's worry. 'Satyavan is too righteous, and his wife, Savitri, even more so. To take Satyavan's life, I must go myself as a sign of respect to him,' said Yama. He mounted his buffalo and left for the forest in the kingdom of Shalva.

The kingdom of Shalva, close to the kingdom of Madra, was ruled by an illustrious king called Ashvapati. He was a man who had brought his senses under control, was magnanimous and committed to the well-being of his people. So he was greatly loved. He, however, had a cause for sorrow, which grew greater every year. He did not have an heir to the throne. One day the worry intensified into a resolve to undertake severe penance, and for eighteen years King Ashvapati followed a rigorous practice worshipping Goddess Savitri. One day his efforts bore fruit and the goddess appeared before him, saying, 'I am pleased with your penance. I will grant you a boon, tell me what you wish.' King Ashvapati had his answer ready. Goddess Savitri also knew what he was going to ask for and she had her answer ready. 'Your desire will be fulfilled. Soon a blessed daughter will be born to you. Desist from replying or remonstrating. Be happy with what you have got.'

The goddess was telling him not to ask for a son, and King Ashvapati did not.

He cherished his daughter, who looked like a divine being born on earth. He named her Savitri. Her beauty went beyond her physical attributes. As she came of age, the father expected neighbouring kings and princes to seek her hand in marriage. But alas, not one came forward. It was apparent, though not articulated, that her effulgence overawed all those who so much as even thought of proposing to her. Finally, an idea came to King Ashvapati. He told Savitri, 'Go forth, my child, taking some of my trusted ministers with you, and tour our kingdom and the neighbouring ones. Look for a suitable match for yourself, and when you find him, come home and tell me so.'

Bashful though she was, Savitri agreed to undertake this tour, for that was what her father wished. When she returned after many weeks, her father was sitting in the assembly, and visiting him was Rishi Narada, the celestial bard.

King Ashvapati was delighted to see his daughter and even more delighted as this meant she must have found a groom. 'Tell me, have you found the right person?' he asked.

'Yes, I have,' said his daughter with a little smile.

King Ashvapati moved to the edge of his throne and said, 'Tell us everything in detail.' And he implored Narada to listen too.

Savitri said:

Ruling the Shalva kingdom once was King
    Dhyumatsena of great might

Though pious and brave, the warrior king one day
 sadly lost his eyesight
That king who had lost his sight had but one son, a
 little child then
When an old enemy usurped his kingdom, sending
 to exile King Dhyumatsena

The king with his little son cradled in the arms of his
 wife
Went to the forest to lead an ascetic life
Born in the city and grown up in the hermitage,
 Satyavan
Is the one, I have accepted in my mind as my partner.[1]

The father's joy at hearing that his daughter had found a suitable match was short-lived, for Narada exclaimed, 'O King! What a grave mistake has Savitri unknowingly committed!' When the king asked him for an explanation, Narada said King Dhyumatsena and his queen were indeed people who lived by Truth and so their son was named Satyavan, the one rooted in Truth. Narada described Satyavan:

Radiant with energy like the sun, wise as Brihaspati,
 the guru of gurus
Courageous as the king of kings and forgiving as
 the earth[2]

The prince is very generous, truthful in speech, devoted, magnanimous, has his senses under control, is gentle but courageous and has a countenance like the moon. King Ashvapati interrupted to ask, 'Where then does his fault lie?'

> He has but one fault, none else
> In a year's time, he has to his body leave[3]

King Ashvapati was shocked. 'This will not do, Savitri. This one drawback obscures all his goodness. Why do you not choose another?' But Savitri said her decision was final. She gave him such convincing reasons that Narada said, 'Savitri has made up her mind. You must go ahead with this.'

King Ashvapati was pensive. But he soon pulled himself together and attended to the next task, which was to visit the exiled King Dhyumatsena. Along with his priests, the king set out on foot to the Shalva forest to meet King Dhyumatsena. King Dhyumatsena was surprised to see King Ashvapati and enquired why he was honoured by his visit.

King Ashvapati said:

> Savitri is the name of my daughter, auspicious and beautiful
> Well versed as you are in dharma, accept her accordingly as your daughter-in-law[4]

King Dhyumatsena was a little taken aback.

> Taken away is my kingdom and forest dwellers we have become
> Living as ascetics, we live by that dharma
> How will your daughter, brought up in luxury
> Cope with this life of hardship?[5]

To this King Ashvapati replied:

> Joy and sorrow are transitory
> This truth my daughter and I know
> So these words spoken are meaningless to me
> Honour my request, please do not refuse[6]

Touched by King Ashvapati's words, King Dhyumatsena not only agreed but added that he had nursed this idea for long but had been unable to ask for Savitri as bride for his son as he was living in difficult circumstances.

The marriage was solemnised, and King Ashvapati went back to his kingdom, leaving his daughter in her new house. Savitri lived happily, bringing joy to her husband and his parents.

> Satyavan was overjoyed to have a wife so full of virtue
> And Savitri too rejoiced at getting a husband of her choice[7]

Savitri rejoiced but kept holding her breath. She knew something that no one else knew and which she could tell no one else. At every smile, at every joy, her mind would taunt her with the deadline, which was only drawing closer by the minute. A year was all she had.

Three days before the fated day dawned, Savitri began an arduous penance, the triratra vow,[8] which entailed fasting for three days and nights. She sought the blessings of Satyavan's parents. 'It is a very difficult vow, all I can say is, may you be successful,' said her father-in-law. The many ascetics who lived in the forest also blessed Savitri, though they did not know why exactly she had undertaken the penance.

And then the fated day dawned. Savitri did not break her fast. She did not want Satyavan to go into the forest alone that day. She wished to accompany him into the forest. Satyavan told her the forest was not easy to navigate. Savitri was persistent. 'For a year I have not stepped out of the ashram, may I have your leave,' she asked Satyavan's father. He was touched that his daughter-in-law should ask him for something and that it was within his powers to grant it. He did caution her that it might be difficult to walk in a forest. Savitri was determined to go and set out with her husband. They walked through the green and luscious forest, abounding in enchanting wildlife. For Satyavan it was a wonderful experience to show the forest to his beloved. 'Look at the peacocks,' he said, 'and the rivers in spate, the trees in full bloom and nature at its best.' Savitri gave him a weak smile in return. Her mind was on what the day was to bring.

> She watched her husband with all his varying
> expressions, but as though dead,
> While the words of the sage hammered within her
> head.[9]

That was when Yama also mounted his buffalo and left for the forest in the Shalva kingdom.

16

Yama arrives in Shalva forest

Satyavan had plucked a whole basket of berries and fruits to take back for his parents. Now he was collecting firewood, when suddenly:

> Approaching his dear wife he said, 'My head hurts
> Perhaps owing to all this strenuous work,
> My whole body is aching, my heart is uneasy
> I think I am unwell, my dear woman of few words.
> I feel like a thousand arrows are piercing my skull
> So I desire to lie down, my dear, I am unable to stand[1]

Savitri's world seemed to stop. Her throat felt dry. She went cold. Had the appointed hour come indeed? She ran towards him and cradeled his head on her lap as he lay down.

> Then that lady of great penance, remembering the prophecy
> Of Narada, calculated the minutes and seconds left[2]

Satyavan lay with his head on her lap. Savitri did not even breathe ... if she held her breath, would that hold time too?

In that scenic forest of trees in full bloom, gurgling rivers, dancing peacocks and singing birds sat this worried and sorrowful young girl who must have still been in her teens.[3] It is said that knowing too much also has its perils. Savitri even knew the exact moment when Satyavan would leave his body ... her heart cried.

Savitri caressed her husband, drew his hair back from his face. He closed his eyes and seemed to have gone off to sleep. The next moment she beheld an apparition standing before her.

> That moment she saw an apparition clad in red silk
> And wearing a magnificent diadem. He was brilliant
> like the sun[4]
>
> With skin of a darker hue, reddish eyes, a noose in
> hand, fear
> He inspired as he stood by Satyavan, and she gazed
> at him[5]

He had arrived. The much-dreaded Yama. The one who had occupied her mind day and night for the past year. The one who was to take away her husband's life.

She hushed her heart, which was pounding, for she was afraid Yama would hear it.

> Beholding him, she gently placed her husband's
> head on the ground
> Bringing her palms together in anjali[6] she rose with a
> trembling heart[7]

Yama was watching her. Though Markandeya[8] has described Yama and what he was wearing, he has not described what Savitri was wearing. Her father had gifted her jewels and silks when she got married. But no sooner had her father left the ashram after her wedding than she had changed into barks and cloth dyed red, as befit a forest dweller. So that is what she must have been wearing, also red, like Yama. Yama saw she was everything he had heard her to be. He could feel her tension. He could see her composure too. Yama normally saw relatives, particularly women, cry and plead. He had seen them lose their mind. This lady stood like a body of penance, radiant and strong. Yama also felt Savitri stood vulnerable in her grief. But her manner of receiving him seemed well rehearsed. She stood up, her beauty enhanced many times over by the aura of the severe penance she was observing.

> That you are a deity is apparent to me from your
> magnificent appearance

> Tell me what you desire, O Lord of the Gods, and
> who you are[9]

Yama smiled. She was asking him to introduce himself! She knew who he was and he knew that. But he realised she was beginning a conversation. He rarely talked with relatives.

> O Savitri, devoted to your husband and full of
> ascetic merit you are,
> So I converse with you. Know me as Yama,
> O auspicious one[10]

Yama was gentle in expression and lavish with his compliments. And he addressed her as the auspicious one, Shubhe, when she was at the point of losing her husband and would normally have been considered inauspicious.[11] What made him feel she was auspicious? Was it her resplendence that stood out despite her grief? Her composure? Her ability to begin a conversation with Death himself? Or did his manner of address show that inherent sympathy and respect he was feeling for her somewhere inside? It was evident that he appreciated her righteous nature, both her devotion to her husband and her pursuit of spiritual merit. But he also saw her as being auspicious, even at that moment when her husband's life was about to go. And traditionally, widows were not considered auspicious.

He had introduced himself modestly and worded the next sentence, which must have been painful for him to deliver, rather carefully. He blurted it out in a rush, self-consciously and as gently as possible.

> Your husband Satyavan of decreased longevity, his soul,
> Binding it in my noose and taking it with me is my purpose[12]

He said many things in those two lines – your husband Satyavan does not have a long life. He has – the Sanskrit term used is *kshina aayu* – a weak life span. So the fault is not mine. I am only taking him where his soul has to go, and that is the duty I have been given.

Here again, it was not of Yama's volition, but his duty, his job, which he is obligated to perform. It was not easy to take the life of a person like Satyavan, and that too in the presence of his very exalted wife. But do it he must, and he had felt strongly that it would be showing due respect to them if he, and not his emissaries, did the job.

It hurt Yama to say these words. He would have liked to reach out to Savitri and assuage her sorrow, tell her explicitly that he was duty-bound, wished he could do otherwise and so on. But he could not do all that. His job was to take Satyavan's life, however difficult it may be to do so. He took a deep breath. Savitri's voice broke his reverie.

I have heard that you send your men to take away
mortals
To take him, Satyavan, why have you come in person,
Lord?[13]

The question delighted Yama. Here was the opportunity he was looking for. He answered with enthusiasm.

He is full of spiritual merit, has a wealth of virtues
and so handsome
To look at; It is not befitting that my messengers
take him, I came myself therefore[14]

No sooner had he spoken than he gasped. What was he doing? Conversing with Satyavan's wife! And explaining his actions? Really, as King of Death, as the supreme in the world of mortality, did he have to explain his actions to Savitri? Yama felt he should quickly finish the job and leave.

Then with his noose he yanked out Satyavan's life
And brought under control that thumb-sized being[15]

Taking that life he had bound in his noose
He turned and proceeded southward[16]

A heartbroken Savitri saw that no sooner had Yama yanked the life out of Satyavan's body than it turned lifeless and ashen. It lost its lustre and that did not make for a happy sight. It tugged at Savitri's heart. But she also saw Yama going ahead. He was carrying the life that was precious to her. She began to follow him.

Yama felt he heard steps behind him. He turned to look, and lo and behold, the lady was following him.

> Turn back, Savitri, and perform the funeral rites,
> your duty
> Towards your husband is complete, you have come
> as far with him as you can[17]

Yama was being matter-of-fact. He had spoken more than was necessary and was now trying to be terse and precise. He commanded Savitri to go back and attend to the matters of cremation.

17

Yama journeys back

As Yama's buffalo Mahisha, also called Paundraka, was trotting on as fast as it could, Savitri tried to keep pace with them, now running, now walking, but maintaining the speed. Where she walked, what the terrain was that led to Yamapuri, was it bright, was it dark, was it cold, was it warm, we do not know. Shri Aurobindo has it thus:

> Luminous[1] he moved away; behind him Death
> Went slowly with his noiseless tread, as seen
> In dream-built fields a shadowy herdsmen glides
> Behind some wanderer from his voiceless herds
> And Savitri moved behind eternal Death
> Her mortal pace was equalled with the god's.

It was a strange experience for Savitri, for she was moving into regions she was unfamiliar with. While Death was moving into lands familiar to him.[2]

We can only imagine the landscape through which Savitri was following Yama. Yama had a long way to go.

His capital city of Yamapuri lay 86,000 yojanas away. The city of Yama, which is spread over a thousand yojanas, is believed to have four entry gates. Through the southern gate go the evil ones. They go to a place where not-so-pleasant conditions prevail. Through the other three gates go the righteous, into a city of splendour and justice. Of these three gates, the western gate is said to be the most superior, and through it enter the mortals who were rooted in truth and possessed all virtues while they lived on earth. So Yama would probably take Satyavan through the western gate.[3]

As Yama was moving on, he felt he heard soft footsteps behind him. He turned back quickly ... yes, she was indeed still following him. She saw him turning back, and so she said:

> Where my husband goes or is being led
> I follow. That is my dharma eternal.[4]

If her lines sound childish and point to a woman peeved, that was not so. Savitri was only giving Yama the opening lines for remonstrating with her ... to say that what she said was true of the time her husband was alive, or something along those lines. Showing her vulnerability, she captured his attention and sympathy. She was showing Yama what mettle she was made of.

> Due to my penance, the blessings of my gurus and my immense love
> For my husband and your favour, nothing can obstruct my way[5]

In just a few words Savitri had told Yama that she had the blessings of her elders, that she had accumulated adequate spiritual merit, that her love for her husband was very strong and, most important, that she had the favour of Yama himself. Yama had never told her so. Now that she, a woman of such rectitude and spiritual attainment, had said so, Yama could not say, 'You don't have my favour.' He did not say anything. He did not know more was to come.

> The wise with true knowledge have said that
> Walking seven steps with another, binds them in friendship.
> From that friendship which I have contracted with you
> I wish to say something and request you to listen[6]

If Yama was disarmed, could one blame him? Referring to the saptapadi,[7] which is the defining feature of the Hindu wedding, Savitri had said that if by walking seven steps you could legalise a marriage, then she had walked more steps behind Yama. He was her friend now. A mere mortal had affirmed her friendship with the king of death. A confident and blessed woman who was not scared of undertaking any journey, however arduous, was now speaking to her friend in Yama, God of Death. And she told him what she thought. Yama was the one who assessed the righteousness of every individual human being. Who better could appreciate what she was going to say:

> There are many who the four ashramas follow
> Of student, householder, forest dweller and
>   renunciate
> But the wise have said true knowledge alone
>   understands dharma
> And so dharma is superior to merely following the
>   four stages
>
> To adhere and live by the dharma of one ashrama
> Is enough to guide one along the right path
> And not desire to pass on to stages one after another
> For dharma is the goal, not the ashramas[8]

Yama was amazed to hear Savitri say all this, though the first thing he said in reply was: 'Turn back.'

Even as he uttered these words, a conversation he had once had with his messengers flashed through his mind. He was instructing them on how they should function and whose lives they should bring bound in their noose. Yama thought, 'When I saw my messengers ready to leave with a noose in their hand, I would whisper a secret to them: The one who knows that everything in this world is but a manifestation of that Supreme One, leave him … do not bring that person bound in your noose.

Just as the earring, crown and bangle look different
Though of the same molten gold made
Similarly, gods, man and animals
Are but manifestations of the one Supreme One[9]

This is true knowledge. When a person has this knowledge, he lives a life of dharma. He does not have to go through the different stages of life and attain wisdom only in the vanaprastha stage of his life.

My messengers asked me how they were to recognise such people who lived by dharma. What I told them in a long conversation has been summarised beautifully by this pious lady in just two sentences. I had told my messengers:

The one who does not deviate from the dharma
That his station in life demands
Maintains equanimity towards friend and foe
Does not take anything that belongs to another
Nor does he take any life

Look upon that person of pure heart and devoid of passion
As the true follower of Vishnu.'[10]

Yama was filled with admiration for this young lady who knew what true knowledge was and that it was independent of outward appearances like ashramas, rituals and symbols. It reflected inner purity. Overwhelmed, he said:

Turn back! Delighted I am with your words
In perfect intonation, diction and reason,
Ask for a boon, excepting his life
And I will grant your heart's desire[11]

Savitri had her request ready. She did not say, 'What would anything mean to me if Satyavan is not beside me?' Instead, she said:

Driven away from his kingdom, in the forest he lives
Losing his eyesight, an ascetic life he has espoused
May my father-in-law regain his sight with your grace
May he be as powerful as the brilliant and radiant sun[12]

Once again Yama was impressed that she had asked for a boon for her father-in-law and granted it immediately. His refrain remained: turn back.

Granted is the boon you desire
As you have wished, so it will happen
You look wearied with this journey
Turn back, do not take any more trouble[13]

As if it would deter her if he moved ahead faster without looking back, as if she would understand his renewed speed as a final goodbye, Yama moved ahead on his path to Yamapuri. Savitiri looked tired as she struggled to keep pace. Yama felt like saying, 'You naive child, can you not see that you can never go to the kingdom of the dead and the dead can never come alive again? Why are you following me? What is your intent? The path is too difficult and you will gain nothing from it.'

This conversation also shows that either the path is arduous in its terrain or the distances have been long.

But wait … was Savitri telling Yama that he was now taking back a life that was living in dharma, the kind of person he had told his messengers not to bring? Yama felt like turning around and telling her, 'Do you not remember, I told you at the outset that I came because your husband was too righteous a man for my messengers to bring. I came to show my respect for him. But that Satyavan had to go was decreed by fate.'

But he did not, for he did not want interaction with her to be encouraged. He wanted Savitri to turn back.

18

Yama and Narayana

Meanwhile, in the Shalva forest the sun was setting. While the sky was still multi-hued, a pall of gloom enveloped the ashrama of Dhyumatsena. Something very surprising had happened. As Dhyumatsena sat on his seat of kusha grass reciting a prayer, he felt he saw a ray of light. 'But I am blind,' he told himself. Slowly and gently, his eyes started receiving more light and he began to get a hazy picture of his ashram. And then he even saw his wife. She had grown old, he thought. But was still comely. Where was Satyavan? Ah! He had gone to the forest to collect wood. But the sun was setting, he should have been home by now.

Overwhelmed, Dhyumatsena walked up to his wife and told her he was getting his vision back. She was amazed, and she too looked for her son to share the happy news with. Their wait began to intensify. Their restlessness grew into obsessive worry. The old couple started going to the other ashrams in the vicinity, asking if Satyavan and Savitri were visiting them.

One small rustle somewhere and they thought their son and his wife had perhaps returned.

Soon ascetics from all the ashramas around and within the forest had assembled at Dhyumatsena's hermitage. They realised the only way to keep Dhyumatsena and his wife calm was to keep them company. Then one of them started telling them a story of a king of yore. Soon many stories came to be shared. Dhyumatsena and his wife would listen engrossed, but suddenly thoughts of their son would pop up and they'd start worrying again.

Savitri's voice came ringing through the air, as if she was pulling his buffalo's reins. Obviously, she was not turning back. Instead, Yama heard her say clearly, in a voice that was chatty though a little breathless:

> Where am I tired? Ha! When I am near my husband,
> how will I be weary?
> As my husband experiences so do I
> Where you are leading my husband, I too will follow
> O exalted king! Do listen to what more I have to say[1]

Yama did not get irritated and say, 'I told you to turn back, why have you not?' He had repeatedly told her to go back. It was more than evident that the final act had been committed … Satyavan's life was now in his noose and Savitri had more years to live. She could not walk into Yamapuri like this. How was he to tell that to this girl? Even though Savitri had come a little too far and Yama wished her to go back, he looked forward to what she had to say next. That was his weakness. He not only loved to live by righteousness but he loved to hear about it. That is why he was also called Dharma or Dharmaraja. This young lady was as articulate as she was wise. She was speaking:

Even a moment spent with the righteous is rewarding
And greater far is their friendship
It is said that such association is never in vain
And so one should always seek it[2]

Yama drew in a breath. Yes, she had said simply that true knowledge is far superior to outward appearances and rituals. And now she was building on that by saying that to be in the company of the wise is the way to be. Without true knowledge, any pious activity is superficial. True knowledge is to know that everything is but a manifestation of the One. Now she was saying that one should live with that Truth, even if not all the time, but strive to do so most of the time. To surrender to It is the ultimate step. She had said all this in the right order. Yama felt like sitting her down by the adjacent rock and sharing an experience with her. His mind started narrating the story as he would tell her:

'Savitri, you will not believe it, but I have seen many instances of what you say unfolding before my eyes. I will tell you of an extreme case of a man who just called out the Lord's name and that itself brought him the rewards of association.

'Once, long ago, there lived a man called Ajamila. One day, while travelling back home from some place where he had gone for work, he had to cross a lonely forest. Before I relate what happened in the forest, I must describe Ajamila's nature of "work". He gambled, stole, cheated and so earned his bread and fed his wife and children. Now in that forest he chanced to see a very attractive woman whose clothes were unsecured and therefore revealing. She seemed inebriated. She eyed Ajamila with desire. Ajamila quickly looked the other way and hastened his steps. The sound of a sigh and the rustle of her garments falling to the ground made him turn back. And then he could never look away after that. He took her for his second wife and she bore him many children. His life, which had never been one of principles, now became even worse.

'Among the many children he had fathered, his youngest he named Narayana. By the time Narayana was born, Ajamila had slowed down with age. All his waking hours were spent in cuddling, feeding and taking care of Narayana.

'And then Ajamila fell sick. He had turned eighty-eight. My messengers arrived at his place, for Ajamila was condemned for all the wrongs he had done in his lifetime, all the hurt he had caused people, mentally or physically, and all the temptations he had succumbed to. Ajamila saw them and felt a pang of fear, not so much for himself as for leaving his little son. "Narayana! Narayana!" he cried in painful agony.

'Guess what happened? The servants of Narayana, the all-pervading Vishnu, landed up there. He had called out to Narayana with such feeling that he had actually summoned the messengers of Vishnu himself.

'"It does not matter even if you say the name in ignorance, but to say the name is enough to purify you," Narayana's messengers said to mine. Now, my messengers were duty bound to bring Ajamila bound in their noose. You know they are the burly type, they are used to getting their way. They see people cower when they appear. Now when they found they were being opposed, the life they had come to take was being protected, they became intolerant. The two sets of messengers got into an argument, and of course the messengers of Narayana won.

'My messengers came to me distraught. "Are you bluffing to us about being the boss or are there many such around?" they asked, bristling. That is when I explained to them the truth that you, Savitri, have just articulated ... even a moment spent in the company of the divine is not without results. In this case, just repeating God's name was enough for Ajamila. As for being your boss, thank you for accepting me as one, but I have a boss above me, above all of us. He is the boss of us all. His will prevails.'[3]

Pleasant it is to take the name of the Lord
To do so the tongue is within our control
Fie! Fie! upon those demonic men
Who don't do so and pave their way to hell[4]

Yama thought he would tell Savitri this with a laugh. 'You know, Savitri, people fear me not because they come to me when they die but because I am not kind to those who are not virtuous or righteous. I am intolerant. How difficult is it to say the name of the Lord? If that can save a person like Ajamila, it can save many others. So I am not able to excuse those who do not live by dharma and in good faith.'

Once many sages were performing a yajna to attain the heavens and one of them wanted to know more about the ways of Yama. The master of ceremonies replied saying that he was willing to describe the way of Yama to those who wanted to hear. The path followed by Yama, he told them, was very difficult to tread. However, for the virtuous ones, the journey would be give happiness. To sinful ones, the journey would be miserable.[5]

Yama had stopped and was staring into space thinking about Ajamila and how people perceived his (Yama's own) duties. He saw that Savitri had come closer. Her determination tugged at Yama's heart. What did she hope to achieve, Yama wondered.

Close to my heart are your words, edifying
To even the wise and learned, your words beneficial
Once again, without asking for Satyavan's life
Ask a second boon, you charming woman[6]

And Savitri was ready with her request. She did not ask for Satyavan's life. It seemed furthermost from her mind, for she said, as soon as Yama asked her to make her request:

The kingdom he had lost, may he regain
The monarch, my father-in-law Dhyumatsena,
That older man I revere as my guru
May he never swerve from the path of dharma[7]

Yama replied:

So be it! His lost kingdom, he will regain
And from the path of dharma he will not swerve
Your ardent desire I have fulfilled
Now turn back, do not exert yourself more[8]

19
How Yama functions

Savitri did not turn back. Yama saw her sitting down. Ah! She is tired, she will turn back now, he thought. But she caught him looking at her and sprang up. She said:

All living beings, you keep under control
In accordance with firm discipline, not your whim
Therefore, it is that you are known worldwide as Yama[1]
Listen further to what I have to say[2]

Eternal dharma means not to bear enmity to anyone
In thought, word or deed, and to nurture
  compassion towards all.
Humans being generally weak and helpless, sages
  like you
Are compassionate even to the enemy who seeks
  refuge in you[3]

Yama's chest swelled with pride. It was not from ego but from a sense of satisfaction that he was achieving what was dear to him: justice. He had an elaborate system of maintaining rhta, or order, in the world. People had to die. True, there were a few times when they did not and Bhoodevi, or Earth, came crying to the Lord seeking Yama's help. Yama decided not to dwell on those episodes now. There is just no escape from dying. That death should have a strong and rational basis is important. Yama kept everything under control with his own superior sense of right and wrong, as Savitri had said. And how does he get all the information needed for this? He has a many layered office functioning in his headquarters. The first level consists of field workers called Sravanas and their wives Sravanis.

Thereafter he (Yama) enquires from Chitragupta of their deeds
Chitragupta, who knows it all, still refers to the Sravanas

The Sravanas, sons of Brahman, wander the earth, sky and netherworlds
Hearing, seeing, even from afar, all that passes, in action, word or thought

Their wives, known as Sravanis, are just like them
They know everything about the doings of women

That which people say or do
Openly or covertly, they report

These eyes and ears of Dharmaraja know the virtue
and vice of everyone
They even know the karma associated with
everyone's word, mind and body

Such is the capability of these who on mortals and
immortals
Have tremendous power
And such is the manner in which
The honest Sravanas convey the matters of men[4]

So the Sravana or Sravani will catch your thought whether you share it with anyone or not. It is then assessed as right or wrong. Their note to Chitragupta would probably look like this: thought of killing husband for a fleeting second, admired colleague's good looks, hated mother, loved mother, gossiped about neighbour, deflated the tyres of the car parked in one's space ... Every emotion and action, negative or positive, is recorded. Sravanas and Sravanis are by everyone's side all the time, so no nuance escapes them.

It is therefore said:

The sun, the moon, the earth, fire, water, sky and
wind, the heart,
Yama, day and night, dawn and dusk, and Dharma
know all the actions of man[5]

Dharmaraja (Yama), Chitragupta, Sravanas, the sun
and others
Are fully aware and assess the merits and demerits of
all beings.[6]

Yama was happy that Savitri understood all this. She understood how many inputs the Sravanas and Sravanis got and how much time the many subordinates of Chitragupta spent adding and subtracting. Only then did Chitragupta come up with the aggregate figures.

However, this lady had the skill of argument. She had begun by saying that if you associated with wise ones, there were always rewards. Now she was saying this was a two-way process – the one who was wise had the ability and the magnanimity to uplift you, even if you were not worthy of it. What to say of the worthy then? Every statement of hers made Yama re-examine his action of binding Satyavan in his noose. Was she suggesting that he show compassion? Compassion could not interfere with duty. She herself had said in her first line that he kept all beings under control and that control emerged from a very calculated order. So she must know that.

Yama then told Savitri:

Words that are like water to the thirsty,
You speak
Ask for another boon
Except the life of Satyavan[7]

Again Savitri responded immediately.

My dear father, the king Ashvapati
Grant him a hundred sons if you may
Through them may his tribe increase
Give me this third boon I pray[8]

Yama granted the boon immediately.

To grow his lineage a hundred sons
I grant to your father, O auspicious one
I have granted your desire for the king father
Now turn back, you have already come too far[9]

Now that she had covered her father-in-law and father, she should be willing to turn back, thought Yama. What more could she want.

Distance I am not aware of since close I am to my husband
My mind indeed is going even further
However, as you are on the move
Listen to the words I have to say

Of the powerful Vivaswat (sun) you are son
Therefore it is that you are called Vaivaswata
You look upon all beings equally
Therefore it is that you are called Dharmaraja

All humans place greater faith
On the wise and virtuous than on themselves
So it is that everyone yearns to develop
And keep their friendship with them

From that friendship is born trust
The wise and the virtuous
Have love for one and all
And so are trusted by everyone too[10]

Yama found Savitri's speech very logical. It flattered him to think she knew so much about him. Just like the sun that shines for all, so too you render impartial service to all, she was saying of him. Savitri had addressed him as Yama and had extolled his virtues as the one who could observe control. Savitri had addressed him as her friend and spoken about how he assessed the deeds of humans, not by their position or status or birth but by their adherence to dharma. She seemed in fact to be reproducing his talk to his messengers. She had addressed him as Dharma and as Vaivaswata. And she had elaborated on his objectivity by saying that because he cared equally for all beings, he took care that justice was done to each birth. This made people respect him, fear him too, for he was invincible. Yama was a tall and broad-built person. He looked taller and broader now.

Pleased, Yama said:

Words you have spoken I have never before heard
From anyone other than you
Indeed I am so happy. Excepting for the life
Of Satyavan ask a fourth boon and I shall give[11]

Savitri was always ready. Pat came the reply. She began softly and then became louder:

With my beloved Satyavan may I
Have a hundred sons, brave and courageous
To continue our family lineage
So I request my fourth boon[12]

Yama replied:

A hundred sons, brave and courageous
They will be and give you great joy
Princess do not trouble yourself further
Turn back, you have come too far already[13]

Savitri was still the same. Not a smile, not a look of victory on her face. Her battle was won, and she knew it. Yamaraja did not. She did not breathe harder, nor did the pitch of her voice rise in excitement. But now no time was to be lost. Savitri, gently and elegantly, gave a very long speech in which she praised the saintly saying they were the true protectors of the world. In a sense, every line of what she said was in praise of Yama as well as an articulation of deep philosophy.

Always engrossed in religion, the saints and sages
Are not mentally disturbed or distressed
Being with them is never fruitless
Following the saintly puts an end to fear[14]

Perhaps Yama felt she was telling him he was being kind, even though she was relentlessly following him. Perhaps Yama felt Savitri was saying that those who adhered to righteous conduct did not have to fear him. This was also true. This was like summarising the nuggets in her conversation from the start.

By their adherence to Truth the saints
Lead the sun on its course
By their constant penance
They sustain the earth
The past, present and the future
Acquire meaning from the saintly
Being in their presence
Destroys people's suffering[15]

Yama was sustaining earth – that was well known. Yama felt the whole verse was in appreciation of him.

Yama is also called Kala, or Time. In the Bhagavad Gita[16] Krishna says that He (Krishna) is Kala, or Time, and then He says: 'I am the great destroyer of the worlds, I have come to annihilate the people. Even without your participation, the warriors on this battlefield will cease to exist.' Time is the one that creates, destroys, resurrects and builds. Indeed, with him, Yama, the past, present and future are defined.

> Knowing this as the eternal way of the good and virtuous
> The saintly devote themselves to the welfare of others, without expectation
> The blessings of saints are never in vain
> Nor does anyone feel inferior or overlooked
> Being with the saints, blessings, self-interest and self-esteem
> Come together, and so the saints are protectors of the world[17]

In death all are equal. The rich and poor die similarly. The blessed and the cursed, both die. Yama felt death was indeed the leveller.

Extremely pleased, but completely oblivious of where the conversation was heading, Yama uttered a few unguarded words. He spoke impulsively and forgot to add the refrain, the caveat.

As you speak, word after word
Meaningful and pleasant to the mind and ears
My respect for you grows more and more
Ask of me some exceptional boon[18]

He did not add 'with the exception of Satyavan's life'. Savitri got her chance.

The boon that you have already bestowed upon me
That boon cannot be fructified (without my husband)
I seek now the boon that Satyavan be brought to life
For without him I am as good as dead
I do not desire happiness without him
I do not desire even heaven without him
I do not desire prosperity without him
I cannot even live without him

You have given me the boon to bear a hundred sons
But you yourself are taking away my husband
Now I pray you grant Satyavan his life
So that your words may come true.

Yama spoke:
Thathastu ... So be it.

20

Yama decides

Yama said it happily and as one would close a hymn, with the finality of an ending and the satisfaction of an achievement. He did not seem surprised or repentant, as he might have been if he thought he had made a mistake. Obviously, Savitri had earned her reward and Yama granted it to her graciously. 'Thathaastu' – his voice, his body, his inner self, all spoke as one, wishing her well. Yama continued:

> 'So be it,' said Vaivaswata Yama, loosening the noose.
> A cheerful and happy Dharmaraja spoke to Savitri thus
>
> O gentle lady, the pride of humanity, your husband I have released
> Take him. Free from illness and ever successful he will be
>
> Both of you will together live for four hundred years
> Satyavan will be known world over as living in his dharma

You will bear with Satyavan a hundred sons, they
Their sons and grandsons will rule the kingdom; in
time
They will be known by your name as Savitra
Your father, Ashvapati, and mother, Malavi
Will have a hundred resplendent sons
And grandsons, all known as Malavas.[1]

Savitri's ears were full. Her heart was full too. She had heard all that she had long hoped to hear. Yama bid her farewell, and this time she did leave. In a trice she was back in the forest of Shalva. Yama too was on his way back home, but he was curious to see how Savitri would get back home. As he watched, she gently placed her ashen-faced husband's head onto her lap. She caressed him and life flowed into him. He opened his eyes with a start. He seemed a little lost.

So long have I slept, why did you not wake me up
Where is that dark-hued person who was dragging
me away?[2]

Replied Savitri:

Yes, indeed you have slept long on my lap
That dark-hued man was Yama, he has now gone
away[3]

Was it a dream or was it real, asked Satyavan of Savitri. But Savitri was now back to her life on earth. She told Satyavan that she would tell him all that later, but now his parents would be getting anxious as it was night. The forest was dark and deep and the cries of wild animals were causing great fear in her, she said.

Yama laughed out loud. 'Look at this girl,' he thought, 'she was not scared of me, of Death. She was fearless as she walked behind me and spoke to me with her head held high and all her senses alert and under control. But now she is scared of wild animals!' And he laughed again. What a woman! he thought.

The forest was dark. How would they find their way home? The thought did come to Savitri and Satyavan that they spend the night in the forest. But Satyavan felt his parents would be very anxious, so they made their way back home. When the thought of their anxiety struck him, his worry knew no bounds. Savitri assured him that if her penance had any value, they would be fine. They both went as fast as their legs could carry them, towards their ashrama.

Dhyumatsena could now experience joy at his eyesight being restored. He saw them and exclaimed in joy. There was great rejoicing in the ashrama when the couple reached home. The many ascetics were still crowding around the older couple. They had been assuring Dhyumatsena and his wife that Satyavan and Savitri would be safe. 'The birds are chirpy, the wind is pleasant,' one of them had said, 'so I am sure Satyavan lives.' Another had said, 'Savitri has undertaken such severe penance. Your eyesight has been restored, I am sure these are good omens and they are safe.' Now, seeing Satyavan and Savitri, all were elated. But they knew nothing of what had happened, and they were intrigued about the restoration of Dhyumastsena's eyesight.

The sage who had observed that it had happened after Savitri's fast of three days and nights asked Savitri what had happened. They all now began questioning Savitri, and she finally spoke:

> Of the appointed time of death, sage Narada had
> foretold
> Today being that day, I did not leave his side
> When he slept, Yama himself came
> And binding him in his noose, went towards the land
> of ancestors
>
> With words that were true I praised the Lord of Death
> He conferred five boons on me[4]

Yama smiled, in fact, broke into a laugh again. She was praising him in words that were true! Savitri was also recounting how she asked for her boons. It amused him. Soon chariots came rolling in to take King Dhyumatsena back to his kingdom. In time, Savitri bore sons. So did her mother. All that Yama had said he would grant Savitri came true.

Savitri's life changed forever. Her meeting with Yama had fulfilled all her desires, whether they were for her parents, her parents-in-law or herself. That, of course, brought much joy. For a year she had lived with Yama on her mind. At that time she lived in fear. After her brush with the infinite, she continued to live with Yama on her mind but with reverence and gratitude.

Was Yama wiping a tear? It was not clear to see. But after the episode, Yama, leaning back in his luxurious home, said, 'Satyavan adhered to his dharma of being a good son, a worthy husband and of living the life of an ascetic with acceptance. Savitri abided by her dharma of choosing her husband and not leaving his side, either because of the prophecy or because of Death itself. And Yama was true to his dharma, he himself went to fetch Satyavan showing his respect for his noble qualities. When everyone follows their dharma zealously, there can never be death, new life resurges.'

Savitri had witnessed and brought about the transformation of the Lord of Death as Life-Giver. Or was it that she had a glimpse of the All-Pervasive One?[5]

Book 6

THE CONCERNED FATHER

21

The life-giver

'Tell me, what can I give you?' asked Yama, God of Death. He was smiling pleasantly at her.

She was disarmed by his question and the manner in which he spoke to her.

Also smiling, a little shyly but very surely, Kunti said, 'A life.'[1]

Thus the God of Death, also called Dharma, known to take lives, gave her a son who became known to the world as Yudhishthira.

Kunti was King Pandu's wife. King Pandu and his two wives, Kunti and Madri, were now living in the forest. Pandu, bound as he was by a curse, could not enjoy marital bliss with either of his wives.[2]

So he had suggested to Kunti that she have a son begat by Dharmaraja himself. Reluctant as Kunti was, Pandu gave her many reasons for why she should have offspring despite his inability to father any. 'Call Dharma, he will not pollute us with sin, nor will his offspring ever nurture sin in his mind.' That is why Kunti had invoked Dharma with special mantras.

These mantras had been given to her by a sage named Durvasa. She had served him well when she was a young girl living in her father's house. Pleased with her sincerity, Durvasa gave her a very powerful mantra by which she could invoke any god of her choice to have children by. It was when she told Pandu that she had such a mantra with her that he advised her to make use of it and bear progeny.

So she had summoned Yama, who had appeared before her, compelled as he was by her powerful prayer. Radiant and resplendent as the sun, he had asked her kindly what he could give her, and upon hearing her reply had granted her a child, a son who was named Yudhishthira.[3]

Many years later, Yama travelled from Yamapuri to earth with a view to meeting Yudhishthira and testing him to see if he was worthy of being his son.

Yama was a good father. His adopted daughter Sunita and her son Vena had learned it the tough way. Sunita and Vena had given him a lot of trouble. Things had become so bad that people began to say that Vena was evil like his grandfather, that he had inherited the dark side of his maternal grandfather, that is, Yama. The gossip did not bother Yama, but Vena's conduct did.

Sunita was a beautiful woman. She was wise and good till one day she went into a forest with her friends and there saw a bright, handsome, young man,

Susanakha, the son of a Gandharva. He was in deep meditation hoping to gain mastery over the art of music. Sunita craved his attention, but he was focused on his dhyana to attain his goal. She provoked him. He told her to go away. She was not deterred. She tried again. He rebuffed her. Gradually, day after day, Sunita's overtures became more aggressive and Susanakha's rebuff of her angrier. She finally thought that it would have an impact if she told the young man how powerful her father was. She told him her father was none other than Yama. Even that had no effect on him. Then she began to abuse him physically. Susanakha was finding it increasingly difficult to tolerate her. Then she hit him in her frustration, but Susanakha remained calm.

One day Sunita came home and reported to her father what Susanakha had told her. 'I struck him, full of anger and love as I was. I told him that my father punishes those who err and protects those who are righteous. To that he made the reply, "One should not beat him who beats one, nor should one make him weep who makes one weep."'

Yama thought his daughter would have understood the nobility of the Gandharva from his response. Indeed, when the one who is attacking is a woman, it is not advised for a man to hit back. Susanakha was being gentlemanly, thought Yama, and was sure his daughter was reporting this to him in appreciation of the young Gandharva. He did not offer any comments. But Sunita was complaining to her father, and when she did not get any reply from him she interpreted it as approval of her behaviour. The next day she went and struck the Gandharva again, and this time he cursed her saying her she would bear a son who would be full of vice. Having cursed her, he moved away.

Now Sunita was shaken. She was greatly disturbed by the curse. She again reported it to Yama, who admonished her. 'Why would you strike a harmless, innocent man practising penance? You have done wrong, Sunita.'

Sunita too was now tormented by grief and regret. Her father told her that just as water makes us calm, cleansed and refreshed, just as fire makes gold shed its impurity, the company of good people and sages washes off sin. 'Practise penance and serve the sages,' Yama advised his daughter. Sunita followed her father's advice and went into the forest to meditate and serve the travelling sages there.

Many days later she met King Anga, who married her. He had been blessed by a sage and told he would have a meritorious son. Vena, the one who scoffed at his grandfather and did all things evil, was King Anga and Sunita's son. When he took over from his father as king, it was the bleakest period on earth. Every living being suffered. Gandharva Susanakha's curse on Sunita was bearing fruit.

Eventually, keeping the company of wise and great sages as per his mother's advice, Vena's sins were washed away and he became a good king. The blessings showered on King Anga were now bearing fruit. So that story ended well. But it had been a long one, and many people had suffered during that period. Earth had to experience a very big resurgence to regain equilibrium.

Now Yama was off to check on his son Yudhishthira. He did not take Mahisha, nor did he dress up in his finery. He flew out of Yamapuri without anyone noticing … as a crane.

In the meanwhile, Yudhishthira had acquired more brothers – Bhima, Arjuna, Nakula and Sahdeva. Kunti had invoked the lord of wind, Vayu, and had a son by him named Bhima. She had invoked Indra, the king of heavens, and had Arjuna. Pandu's younger wife, Madri, too wished to bear children. The gracious Kunti had taught her the mantra too. Madri invoked the Ashvins, twin sons of Surya and Sanjna, to give birth to Nakula and Sahdeva.

As the years passed, these five boys grew up, married Draupadi and were in Dvaiytvana when Yama was going towards them.

22
The yaksha

The Pandavas – Yudhishthira, Bhima, Arjuna, Nakula and Sahdeva – along with Draupadi, were resting in Dvaiytvana when a brahmin came to them seeking help. 'My two fire sticks and the kindling rod got stuck on the horns of a deer when it butted its head against them. The deer ran away when it saw me approaching and carried with it my fire twigs and the rod. Those things are essential for me to keep my spiritual practice going. Can you help retrieve them for me?'[1]

The Pandavas immediately sprang to action, and seeing the deer at a distance began to chase it. They went a long distance, but suddenly the deer disappeared. Having failed in their attempt to get back the brahmin's possessions, they sat down exhausted under the shade of a banyan tree. The sun was sharp and the chase had been long. The Pandavas were thirsty.

'Nakula,' said Yudhishthira, 'will you climb up this tree and, looking in all ten directions, see if there is a waterbody anywhere about? Your brothers are tired and thirsty.'

Nakula did as he was told. 'I see a lake with many trees around it, and I hear the cries of sarus cranes. So there must be water there.'

Yudhishthira was delighted. He told Nakula to take the quiver and get some water for his brothers. Nakula went. Time passed. He did not return. The brothers' thirst was intensifying, the wait seemed interminable. So Yudhishthira sent Sahdeva to check why Nakula had not yet returned. Sahdeva left for the lake.

Amid all the Sarus cranes stood Yama in the guise of a crane. He wanted Yudhishthira, and there was only one way to get him. So he set in motion the following events.

As soon as Nakula reached the banks of the lake and saw the pure, clear waters he bent down to cup some water in his hands. Just then a voice called out to him and he saw it came from a crane. It said, 'Stop! Do not dare to partake of these waters, which are mine, before answering my questions.'

Nakula did not have the energy to even glance towards the crane. He needed water first. He was too strong to be slayed by any, so without paying heed to the voice, he took a mouthful and soon fell down, as though dead.

That is how Sahdeva found his brother. He was shocked to see his brother lying lifeless on the ground.

The voice called out to Sahdeva too. 'Stop! Do not dare to partake of these waters, which are mine, before answering my questions.' Sahdeva paid no heed. He could see and hear nothing but water, and he too had just put the water from the lake to his lips when he fell down, as though dead. Yudhishthira, Bhima and Arjuna waited and waited, until Yudhishthira looked at Arjuna, who stood up immediately and went in search of his brothers Nakula and Sahdeva. Arjuna saw a desolate landscape but for a few cranes. He saw his brothers sprawled on the ground. Tired he already was, but now, on seeing the lifeless forms of his brothers, he also felt greatly anguished and disturbed. His anger rose. 'Who had the audacity to do this!' his mind screamed. A mouthful of water first, he thought, and strode angrily towards the lake. The same voice that had addressed his brothers said the same thing to him. 'Stop! Do not dare to partake of these waters, which are mine, before answering my questions.'

Arjuna's anger could not be controlled. He looked around and said, 'Appear before me and prevent me if you can. Do not speak to me from hiding. I will finish you with my arrows.' His face was red and his breath short. He shot arrows in every conceivable direction and then bent down to sip some water. The voice warned him again, but uncaring as Arjuna was, he took a mouthful. He fell dead.

Yudhishthira then sent Bhima. Bhima roared when he heard the crane's warning. He was ready to fight with whoever was threatening him. Sheer muscle power blocked his vision. And so the same fate befell him. Finally, Yudhishthira himself came. Yama was happy! He was breathless with excitement to see how his son would react to his warning.

Yudhishthira was shocked and grieved to see all his brothers lying lifeless on the ground. He went to each of them, cradling them in his arms and crying.

> … and began thinking, by whom have these
>   warriors been slain?
> There are no marks of weapons on their bodies
> Nor are there footprints around the bodies
> He must be someone of super strength
> Who has my brothers slain
> Focusing on it, my answer I will find
> After partaking of some water to quench my thirst[2]

He had to find out how this had happened. Could there be anyone more courageous and stronger than his brothers? Yudhishthira was unbelieving of what seemed to have happened. And yet he could see them with his own eyes, limp and lifeless. Somewhere, things were not as they appeared, he felt. Bent with sorrow, he walked to the lake to cup some water in his hands and put them to his lips when the same voice sounded. It said:

I am a crane, feeding on moss and fish
I have taken your brothers to the grasp of death
You will be the fifth victim, O Prince
If you too do not answer my questions.
Dear child, do not be rash and try
For these waters are already mine
Answer my questions
And thereafter by all means drink or carry water

Yudhishthira listened with humility and asked:

Are you the head
Of Rudras, Vasus or Marutas?
I ask you to tell me who you are Lord
For a mere bird could not have done this

Himavan, Priyatra, Vindhya and Malaya
Four mountain-like figures were felled by whom?
Few can face them, let alone win over them
You have done a great job
I do not know what you do, nor why you do it

Excited and curious am I
Frightened too

My heart is distressed and my head dazed
I ask you therefore to tell me who you are and why
you are here

Yama smiled. Even in such anguish as Yudhishthira was, peering over each brother and exclaiming that since their complexion had not changed they could not have been poisoned, he chose his words well. Yama answered him:

A yaksha I am
Not an aquatic bird, the crane.
I have killed them
All your powerful brothers

And then the yaksha revealed himself. He was a huge and heavily built being with unnaturally bulging eyes. He towered above the palm trees and was brilliant like the sun, with a voice as deep as thunder. He spoke from the treetop again.

These brothers of yours, O King! Despite my
warnings,
Disregarding me, partook of the waters and so I
killed them
He who loves his life O King
Should not venture to drink this water

Their possession (of the water) has been obtained by me
And so answer my questions and by all means
Drink and take away as much water as you wish

Yudhishthira was but a small speck on the ground against the towering yaksha. He replied with composure:

No desire have I to partake of
That which is someone else's.
Virtuous men never indulge such desires
Nor do they sing their own praise
I will answer your questions
To the best of my knowledge

Yama was pleased. The beginning was promising. And he began with his first questions:

Who leads the sun to rise and who are those around the sun?
Who leads the sun to set? And in what is the sun established?

Yama began at the very beginning, or do we say at the very end? Yudhishthira was ready with the answer:

It is Brahma who makes the sun rise.
Celestials hover around the sun.

It is Dharma which leads the sun to set
And Surya is established in Truth.

Yama was happy with the answer. He, Yama, always maintained that the highest and the most basic learning was that everything was but One. There is a higher universal intelligence that makes the world tick. And the sun symbolises truth, knowledge and enlightenment. When it rises, it is His grace. Having spoken of his father, the next question Yama asked was about himself: what causes the sun to set? Just as the sun rises, it has to set to rise again – that is the cyclical order of life. Similarly, life has to meet death to return to life. And Yama had waited to hear what Yudhishthira said, 'Dharma causes the sun to set . . .' As Yama had always maintained, if one follows one's dharma, the transition from life to death and back again is smooth and happy. What is dharma? That itself is dharma; in this context, impermanence, that which rises has to set, that which lives has to die.

He had met many who knew all this theoretically but did not know how to put it into practice. Remembering Rishi Gautama at this point, Yama asked Yudhishthira:

What makes one learned?
With what does one attain greatness?
By what does one obtain a second chance?[3]
And how does one become wise?

Yudhishthira answered:

> Through shruti one becomes a shrotriya,[4]
> Austere penance brings greatness.
> Support and perseverance[5] give one a second chance.
> Wisdom is gained by service to elders.

Yama was brimming with pride on hearing his son's answers. Yudhishthira had rightly pointed out that learning and penance are important. Life should never be viewed as 'hopeless', because one can always avail of a second chance at turning one's life around by keeping the company of wise men and serving them. So true learning is that which is reflected in good conduct towards fellow beings. This may sound easy and simple, but Yama knew that even after several years of penance, Rishi Gautama had failed to figure this out. Rishi Gautama lived on Mount Pariyatra. He practised austerities for sixty thousand years. This man of such evolved spiritual merit had a doubt. When Yama went to clear his doubt, Gautama could feel and realise the presence of Yama because of the austerities he had practised.

Bowing to Gautama, the bull among men, Yama asked, 'Tell me, what can I do for you?'

Gautama asked, 'How can one exhaust one's debts to one's parents? How can a man quickly obtain the radiant worlds which are so difficult to obtain?'

Yama replied, 'Austerities, purity, constant devotion to truth and dharma, worship of parents day after day, these are the tasks one should be attached to.'[6]

In the first set of questions about how the world awakes and sets, about what makes all that happen, Yama was asking about the macro picture. The second was to the individual. How does the individual attain moksha? Yama asked this single question as two shorter ones. The answer to the first was that one became learned by internalising the shruti texts. That was important because knowledge is what removes the veil of ignorance. Once knowledge is gained, severe penance clears up the remaining fog, and greatness can be achieved. In spiritual matters, attaining moksha is attaining greatness.

The second part of the questions was how does get a second chance and how does one become wise. Constant practice, there is no finishing line, alone gives a second chance, and service alone brings wisdom. This is exactly what Gautama had wanted to know when he had asked the above questions. Yama had told him service to his parents is lifelong, for that alone will bring wisdom.

In his first set of questions, Yama had asked Yudhishthira about the macro picture. Now he wanted to know the details. Whichever way it is worded, the question is the same: how to attain the heavens, moksha, Brahman, call it what you may. Rishi Gautama had called it the radiant world. Yama asked Yudhishthira how to attain greatness. Greatness in spiritual matters is achieved only by attaining Brahman, was the reply. Yama had asked the question in two stages so as to lead Yudhishthira to the right answer. Ignorance is the veil over knowledge. Once knowledge is sought, which can happen by internalising the shruti texts, severe penance clears up any remaining fog. Gautama observed that however much one serves one's parents, the sense of gratitude only increases. Gautama was overwhelmed. So he asked Yama if there could come any time when one could stop worshipping one's parents. 'No,' Yama had replied, 'it has to be lifelong service.'

23
Yama and Arjuna

The yaksha did not become any more pleasant in appearance, even though he was happy with the answers Yudhishthira was giving him. He remained huge and menacing, but Yudhishthira looked relaxed. He was perhaps at ease now that he knew the type of questions he would have to answer. It is true that a sip of water would have made it easier for him, but ...the yaksha was now asking him another lot of questions:

What is it that makes a brahmin godly?
What dharma do brahmins share with the virtuous?
What is that makes them ordinary humans?
What trait do they share with those without virtues?

Yudhishthira responded immediately:

Their swadhyaya[1] is their divine or godly aspect
They share their ascetism with the virtuous
Mortality is their human trait
Slander is a trait they share with the virtues-less.

Yama took a deep breath. How accurately Yudhishthira had answered. Once Yama had been faced with a difficult situation. It was not to do with slander really, but, thought Yama, it was misconduct of the same genre. A brahmin ascetic by the name of Kaushika had once been brought to him by Chitragupta. 'This man,' Chitragupta had told him, 'lived at the confluence of two rivers and vowed to always speak the truth. One day a group of people, fearing robbers who were chasing them, happened to run into the forest area where he was residing. They sought refuge in him and ran into a side of the forest which had dense greenery. Soon the robbers themselves came into the forest and, spotting Rishi Kaushika, went up to him and asked if he had seen a few men run past.' Since Kaushika had resolved to adhere to the truth, he told them what direction the group had gone in. The robbers soon found them and not just robbed them but also killed them. Should this man, who was not discerning but wedded to truth and performing severe penance, go to hell or heaven?[2]

To Yama the answer had been simple, but he was aware that the story of Kaushika would be used by many as a touchstone for righteousness and so pondered over it a little longer and said, 'He goes to hell.' When Chitragupta asked him why, Yama replied, 'One is to be conversant with morality to be able to distinguish between truth and falsehood.

Truth uttered without righteousness is better not spoken at all. Kaushika betrayed the trust placed in him, sharing knowledge which led to the loss of lives.'

The yaksha now asked the next set of questions:

What is divine in kshatriyas?
What dharma do they share with the virtuous?
What is their human trait?
And what trait do they share with those without virtues?

Yudhishthira was quick with his response:

Arrows and weapons are their divine aspect
Their willingness to sacrifice themselves they share with the virtuous
Fear is their human trait
Desertion is the trait they share with those without virtues

In a fleeting minute a whole drama enacted itself before Yama's eyes. The scene of Arjuna practising austere penance for weapons and arrows to equip himself to fight the Mahabharata war. It happened when the Pandavas were preparing for war against the Kauravas. One day Yudhishthira called Arjuna and told him that Duryodhana was very strong in terms of his army and resources. He was being nice to all his warriors and winning their loyalty. The revered ones were taking either his side or no side at all. The odds were against them, the Pandavas, and the onus was on Arjuna to win the war for the Pandavas. 'So,' said Yudhishthira to Arjuna, 'go to the forest, practise severe ascetism and gain the favour of Siva and other deities. You must collect weapons and arrows from all the deities and powers that be.'

Arjuna did as he was told, and soon Siva Himself appeared before him, and thereafter many other deities. Three celestials came together – Varuna, associated with water; Kubera, the god of wealth; and Yama, the lord of justice. Varuna came as a dazzling gem, accompanied by aquatic animals. Kubera, with a body that resembled pure gold, came seated in a splendid vehicle, accompanied by many yakshas. When Yama came, elegant and powerful, all the three worlds lit up. The destroyer of the worlds came along with those who nurture it.

Singing Yama's praise they said:

The one who has the power to destroy it all
The God of Justice upon whom it is impossible to
  meditate
Came in his chariot, mace in hand, lighting the three
  worlds
Of Guhyakas, Gandharvas and Nagas[3]
Like a second sun at the end of a yuga

Varuna, Kubera and Yama saw Arjuna in meditation on the mountain, and that is where they had come.

Thereupon the highly erudite and pious Yama
With a voice like that of the rumbling cloud
Who lived in the southern region
Said as follows to Arjuna, the warrior

O Arjuna, behold, all the protectors of the Universe have come
We will enable you to see us, as worthy you are of our sight
By the blessings of Brahma, you are now born mortal
You were once Nara, a sage of infinite prowess

You will vanquish the highly respected and virtuous Bhishma
You will also defeat the kshatriyas of fiery energy
And you will slay Karna who is a portion of my father
Marthanda, who lights up all regions

The demons and monsters born on earth
Will be slayed by you
And attain to such regions
As their acts decide they should

The earth shall be lightened of her burden by you along with Vishnu
O Mahanubahu![4]

Accept this weapon of mine, this mace
Which cannot be countered
With it, accomplish great deeds you will.[5]

Arjuna received the weapon, the mantra and rites associated with it and the means of hurling it and withdrawing it. After Yama, Varuna and Kubera gave their weapons to Arjuna, they all returned to their abodes.

Yama appreciated Arjuna's unhesitating undertaking of severe penance to acquire these weapons. It was his penance that had won him the weapons. Indeed, they are the divine aspects of kshatriyas. Perhaps, thought Yama, Yudhishthira was also recollecting this scene when he was answering him.

24
Yama as a calf

Yama saw Yudhishthira looking up at him waiting for the next question. Not once had he glanced towards the water. Yama was proud that his son was so strong. He sent forth a volley of questions and the replies were immediate.[1]

The yaksha laughed. Yudhishthira smiled. Theirs was a quick exchange.

The yaksha looked visibly relaxed. He now sent a new volley of questions Yudhishthira's way:

> What is the most valuable among all that which
> descends? What brings the greatest benefit when
> it is sown in the earth?
> What is the best among all that which is established?
> What is of greatest value among those who speak?

Yaksha's questions were not as simple as they sounded. He was testing Yudhishthira's knowledge of the Vedas. But Yudhishthira was prepared. He answered:

Rain is the most valuable among all that which
descends, the seed brings greatest benefit when it
is sown
The cow[2] is the most valuable for those who seek
prosperity, a child[3] is of greatest value in the
world of those who speak.

Yama was pleased. Indeed, rain symbolises both water and the abundance of heaven. Rain has elsewhere been described as the waters gathered by the sun. Their pouring down is to bring to the earth the luminous light of the heavens.[4]

The cow was literally a sign of physical wealth. Symbolically, it stood for light and knowledge, both of which were required for prosperity. Yama's head was brimming with thoughts of a time when Earth had been ravaged and life on Earth needed to be revived. He wanted to ask Yudhishthira casually, 'Do you know of the times I took the form of a calf and the milkman?' When King Vena, his grandson, had wreaked havoc on Earth, Earth had swallowed up all her assets. Then Yama's great-grandson Prithu became king. But the world was still in a mess. Rising up to help him, Earth said, 'Everything is in a mess because evil ruled the world. Herbs and plants, which were created by Brahma, are being enjoyed by the wicked who have not undertaken religious observances. When I was left unprotected and uncared for by rulers, and when the world was infested with thieves, I swallowed those herbs and plants to preserve them within me for the performance of sacrifices. As a long period has lapsed since then, those plants and herbs within me have become diminished and weak. You should, therefore, try to take them out by some expedient known to be effective in such matters. O mighty-armed hero! O protector of creatures! If Your Lordship desires to provide nutritious food coveted by creatures, please arrange for a calf, a suitable vessel and a milkman competent to draw milk, so that, being full of affection, I shall yield for you all your desired objects in the form of milk, O warrior. O mighty king! Make me a level plain so that the waters showered by Indra may stand on me, even after the rainy season is over.'[5]

Prithu did as Earth bid him, and everyone took turns to be the calf, the milker and the milk pot. Each of them got their powers back. When the yakshas milked, they got the power to disappear at will as milk in an unbaked pot. Human beings milked Earth for crops and cultivation. Seven rishis milked Earth and got the Vedas as their milk. The Pitris, or ancestors, milked Earth, getting Swaha. Swaha became the wife of Agni. Swaha is an aspect of Agni without whom it is believed Agni cannot be. Every oblation ends with the auspicious word 'swaha'. Swaha invokes the deity, and mantras generally refer to the deity and swaha is added after the deity's name. For example, *Angnaye swaha* literally means a good or auspicious invitation to Agni. So when the Pitris milked Earth and Swaha emerged, Yama was the calf and the milkman.[6] That brought new life to Earth. It was like a resurgence of prosperity.

25

Yama, Yayati and Yamuna

Though Yama was the one asking questions of Yudhishthira, his head was so full of thoughts that he was afraid he would lose track of what he was asking his son. With each question, memories flooded his mind. But he saw Yudhishthira waiting. Quickly he asked him a simple question to buy time and calm his own thoughts:

> Who is the one who lives actively by his senses
> Is intelligent, is worshipped by the world
> Is respected by all and breathing evenly
> But not alive?

Yama had just about finished asking the question and Yudhishthira began answering it.

> The one who does not offer service
> To the Lord, to guests, to servants, to ancestors
> Or to himself, is breathing but
> Is not alive.

Yudhishthira's quick answer brought Yama's mind back to the present. Again, a quick volley of questions came hurtling at Yudhishthira. The Pandava, whose body had become a little limp, now perked up. The real cranes started calling, as though even they understood.

Yama: Who is greater than the earth?
Yudhishthira: The mother is greater than the earth.

Yama rejoiced inwardly. He too thought so. His mother had been very loving and caring. That was why, when Chhaya, standing in for his mother, cursed him, he was sure she was not his mother. Quickly Yama asked the next question:

Yama: Who is superior to the sky?
Yudhishthira: The father is superior to the sky.

'Yes, indeed,' said Yama joyously. His father Surya was literally also the loftiest!

Yama: What is swifter than the wind?
Yudhishthira: The mind.
Yama: What is more numerous than grass?
Yudhishthira: Thought, particularly those thoughts that are disturbing.

The yaksha held his breath. Indeed, so many thoughts and of so many different kinds, distracting, worrisome, alluring ... and the mind hops from one to another. Not just hops, changes too. It is strange, thought Yama, that the best of men have fallen prey to the mind's fickleness. He remembered King Yayati.

Yayati was a good ruler. He had instructed all his people to be devout followers of Vishnu. 'Restrain yourself. Pursue only truth. Utter only the Lord's nectar-like name,' the king told his countrymen, and followed it up with detailed instructions, also informing the people that those who did not follow them would be punished. Soon the people of his kingdom were so righteous and devout that Yama had a problem.

Yama went straight to Indra. Indra greeted him warmly and asked why he had come. 'The son of Nahusa, that is, Yayati, has made everyone in his kingdom a follower of Vishnu and his kingdom has become like Vaikuntha. The six vices of anger, lust, greed, jealousy, desire and ego have vanished from his kingdom. No one tells lies or commits sin. They do good work with the name of Narayana on their lips. This means they are all very healthy and fathers have had sons, grandsons and great-grandsons and are still alive.'

'How wonderful,' exclaimed Indra, and both Indra and Yama spent a moment in silence imagining that beautiful kingdom. Breaking the silence, Yama spoke,

'There is a problem. No one is dying. So, Indra, I have nothing to do! I am free.'

Indra knew of King Yayati. 'I sent my messenger Matali to invite Yayati to heaven, but he told him that he would create a heaven on earth and has no need for this heaven!' replied Indra, rubbing his chin.

'Well,' said Yama, 'bring him here. You have to or else you will invite more problems ...'

Indra thought deeply and then called for Kama (Cupid) and his wife Rati. He told them to target Yayati. Kama and Rati set off on their new assignment. They went as stage artistes and sought to perform before King Yayati. The lady sang so beautifully that Yayati was attracted to her. A day after the performance, still a little heady with the feeling of attraction he had experienced, he went out into the forest to hunt. There he heard a melodious song. The trap Kama and Rati had set up for him worked. So mesmerised was he by the voice that he went in the direction from where it came. He eventually came to a pond with beautiful blue waters and surrounded by flowers of all colours. There he saw a maiden sitting on a rock in the middle of the pond. He was captivated by her. He asked her who she was. The young woman told her friend to make the introductions, which she did. Yayati understood the maiden was looking for a suitable groom, and he seemed to fit all her specifications. 'Why not consider me?' asked the impassioned king. The friend took the proposal to the beautiful maiden. She got a reply from her, which she passed on to the king. 'You are perfect in everything, but you are old,' the friend observed. Yayati went back and traded his old age for his son's youth. He then married that lady and lived happily for some years thereafter.[1]

Yama recollected this story because he had been instrumental in tempting Yayati in an indirect way. How Yayati's mind had been so fickle as to give up all the merit he was accumulating just for a little temptation … He lost heaven for lust! That is the nature of the mind.

In order to emphasise that, Yama asked Yudhishthira the next set of questions:

> Yama: What does not close its eyes when it sleeps?
> Yudhishthira: The fish does not close it eyes when sleeping.

Yama thought he would outwit Yudhishthira. But Yudhishthira was too clever. Why would Yama ask about a fish's sleeping habits in the middle of a serious philosophical discussion? Yudhishthira knew the fish symbolised vigilance and awareness even in states of rest. Just as the sleeping fish represents alertness in a state of calm and repose, Yudhishthira was alert to this question. The open eyes of the fish are a message to the observer to be mindful. They are also a reminder that even though you may sleep, time is ticking constantly. Or Yama is watching. Whether you sleep or whether you hide in a cave, Yama keeps his watchful eyes on you, and when your time is to be up, it will be. So a wise person should be like the fish, ever alert and aware of his or her spiritual path, and be vigilant and mindful. Yama was happy Yudhishthira knew he did not stop for sleep or rest ... he was always on the move, which was why he was also called Kala. And that is possible only when there is stillness of the mind. The sleeping fish represent thoughts that do not disturb the tranquil lake of a wise person's mind. That is why he asked the next two questions in quick succession:

> Yama: What does not move when it is born?
> Yudhishthira: An egg does not move on being born.
> Yama: What does not have a heart?
> Yudhishthira: A stone does not have a heart.

Both the egg and stone are still. One is full of potential, the other dense. One is life, the other inert. To nurture life, you need a heart and you need momentum. Momentum brings with it renewed vigour. So Yama asked:

> Yama: What increases due its own speed?
> Yudhishthira: A river swells with its own speed.

With every mention of a river, Yama would think of his twin flowing untiringly and unceasingly as Yamuna on earth. Yama met her occasionally, when he went that way. Once, on the second day of the dark fortnight in the month of Kartika (15 October to 14 November), Yama felt he wanted to see Yamuna and went to visit her.

He was so moved by the thought of his sister that he impulsively released many souls that were in less pleasant environs in hell. They were surprised to be released. They did not expect it. But Yama felt that perhaps this gesture of kindness would sow the seeds of compassion in their hearts, perhaps making them better human beings in their next birth.

Yamuna too was delighted to receive her brother and to hear of his act of releasing the unhappy people from their hell. She showered him with love, as sisters do when their brother comes home. She cooked for him, pampered him, applied a red mark, the tilak, on his forehead and served him delicacies she had prepared with care.

The day ended too soon and Yama had to get back. He hugged his sister and said, 'Thank you for being so kind and loving to me. Tell me if I can do something for you.'

Yamuna did not have to think. 'May this day be celebrated by all brothers and sisters. May this become the ritual that the brother visits the sister, she serves him good food after applying the red tilak on his forehead and prays that her brother will be free from fear of you. Fear of Yama.'

'So be it,' said Yama and till today people celebrate that day as Bhaiya Dooj, after the festival of Deepavali. 'Let me add to it. I will also not take anyone who bathes in your waters.'

So, on the day of Bhaiya Dooj every sister prays to a benevolent Yama, who is bound by his promise to bless the brother with a long life.[2]

Since Yama was thinking of relationships, his next few questions were on those lines.

26

Yama and Nrga

Once, when Yama was travelling, he heard the roar of a wild animal and saw it racing towards a small camp of travellers in the forest. The roar sounded terrifying, and generally such sounds came when his visit was due. But Yama paused as he reflected and checked ... No. No soul was to be carried away from this forest. So he waited to see what was going on.

A merchant had undertaken a journey to a faraway kingdom to sell his goods. On the way, he had met three fellow travellers: a donkey, a dog and a rooster. They had agreed to travel together, helping one another along the way. The donkey offered to carry the merchant's baggage. The rooster served as their morning alarm so they kept to time and travelled when it was still daylight. The dog kept guard at night.[1]

Now, as Yama was watching the wild animal racing towards the group, the dog started to bark. The merchant woke up and quickly lit a fire. That scared the animal, which went away quietly. So Yama was not required to intervene.

On his return along the same way, Yama saw the group again. The merchant had sold his wares and had shared his profits equally among his friends.

Yama now asked Yudhishthira:

Who is a friend in foreign lands? Who is the friend at home?
Who is the friend of the ailing? What is the friend of the dying?

Yudhishthira answered all four questions:

Travelling companions are the friends in foreign lands
The spouse[2] is the friend at home
The healer[3] is the friend of the ailing
And charity is friend of the dying.

Yama had once been cursed by a sage. His body had started experiencing a burning sensation after that. No remedy worked. Yama applied sandal paste and had several perfumed showers. But nothing brought him relief. Yama became restless and agitated. He prayed to Siva, who blessed him and told him to bathe in a particular pond, which became known as Yamateertham in later years. That dip cured Yama,[4] and he was happy again. Indeed, he recollected with gratitude the divine healer who restored his health to him.

Yama had once asked his messengers to get him a pious brahmin named Sharma, and the messengers, by mistake, brought another brahmin equal in merit. The brahmin who had been brought wanted to stay on, but Yama said it was not within his control to cut short his duration on earth and he was sent back. But before that, the brahmin Sharma was also brought. To both, Yama explained that acts of charity, like serving water to people, getting wells and lakes dug, making donations and lighting lamps in dark areas, were among the most virtuous acts that one could perform. The brahmin Sharma was also sent back to earth, and both brahmins followed Yama's instructions for the rest of their lives.[5]

Yama was about to ask his next question to Yudhishthira when an episode to do with King Nrga came to his mind. He felt like telling Yudhishthira to add the word 'mindful' before charity. Mindful charity is the friend of the dying.

There had lived, some time ago, a good and righteous king called Nrga. One day a cow from a brahmin's house joined King Nrga's herd of cows and was brought back to the palace along with the other cows that belonged to the king. The owner of the cow searched here, there and everywhere but could not find his cow. King Nrga was meanwhile engaged in donating cows to brahmins with a view to attaining the heavens. Unknowingly, of course, he gave away the cow that was not his too. But its owner brahmin saw his cow with the brahmin who had received it in donation from the king. He called out to his cow by her name, Shabali. The cow responded and came to him. He then went to the king and complained that the king had donated a cow that did not belong to him. That was a mistake. But the new owner of the cow refused to return the cow. Neither brahmin agreed to the king's offer of many more cows in place of Shabali. Both cursed Nrga, saying he would turn into a lizard. So when Nrga went to Yama, Yama told him, 'In your resplendent character profile, there is one blemish. What happened?' King Nrga told him the story. 'Well,' said Yama, 'you can either face your punishment first or enjoy your rewards first. Choose.' King Nrga chose to serve his period of punishment first. Instantly he felt himself falling to the ground and into a well, where he lay as a huge lizard. During his free fall, he heard Yama's words, 'Krishna will save you.' It was when Vishnu incarnated as Krishna that King Nrga's period of punishment got over and he ascended to the highest of heavens, where he sits in Yama's court adulating him.[6]

To be constantly aware of one's actions is important, reflected Yama. A little laxity and much is lost. That thought made him ask more questions.

Who is everybody's guest? What is the religion that
is eternal?
O great king! What is known as amrita? What is the
entire Universe?

Yudhishthira was ready with his answer:

> Agni is everybody's guest, the light of divine bliss
> (Soma) is the amrita
> Ananda is the eternal religion and the Lord of Life,
> Vayu is this entire universe.[7]

Yama was impressed with Yudhishthira because he could see that Yudhishthira saw the larger picture. Agni or Jatavedas is the energy of the life force. He is the power, the Will. Though soma is commonly understood as an intoxicating drink, what can be more intoxicating than a brush with the divine? Yama thought of his father Surya, the moon, Agni and asked:

> What is it that travels alone? What is it that is born
> again after its birth?
> What is it that mitigates the cold? What is the largest
> field?

Yudhishthira answered:

> The sun wanders alone, the moon is reborn again
> and again
> Fire combats the cold and the earth is the largest field.

27

Yama and Nala

To emphasise that even though one may perform one's dharma diligently, as King Nrga did, one has to be ever alert, Yama asked Yudhishthira another set of questions:

> What is the single thing needed to attain dharma?
> What is the single thing needed to attain fame?
> What is the single thing needed to attain heaven?
> What is the single thing needed to attain happiness?

Yudhishthira replied:

> All-round capability is important in the discharge of
> one's duties to attain dharma
> Charity is the only thing that can bring fame,
> Truth is the single most important step to heaven
> And good conduct alone results in happiness.

Yama understood from Yudhishthira's response that he had heard the story of Nala, son of King Virasena.

When Arjuna went to the forest to undertake penance to get arms and weapons, Yudhishthira, his wife and brothers had been feeling depressed. Rishi Brihadashva was visiting them and Yudhishthira, in a fit of despondency, said, 'I don't think there is another man who has faced so much misfortune.' Rishi Brihadashva told them the story of Nala. Yama recollected the first part of the story, where he had been involved too.

Narada, the celestial bard, visited Indra and told him that Damayanti's swayamvara was to take place soon. Damayanti, daughter of the king of Vidarbha, was known for her beauty and elegance. Suitors from all over the world were vying for her hand. At the very time Narada was announcing this, Agni, Varuna and Yama arrived at Indra's court. All of them decided to participate in the swayamvara. Dressed in their best, they came down to earth and headed towards Vidarbha. Nala too had set out to attend the swayamvara. The celestials saw him and thought, 'In beauty he is like the personification of Kama himself. He is resplendent as the sun.' They approached him and asked him if he would be their messenger. Nala was taken aback. He did not even know who they were, and they were asking him to be their messenger. The celestials introduced themselves, and Nala agreed to be their messenger. Now they revealed their message: they told him that they were going to Damayanti's swayamvara and wanted him to tell her to choose one from among the four of them. 'When I too have set out on the same purpose, how can I promote your cause?' asked Nala. He had been in love with Damayanti for a long time now, though he had never set his eyes on her. What he had heard about her was enough.

'But you promised us you would be our messenger, so you are bound by that promise,' they said. That was true. Nala had made his promise without checking what message was to be delivered, and to whom. He was now left with no choice. He had to stand by his word.

'How will I gain entry into the palace which is so well guarded?' asked Nala.

'You will,' said Indra, with the authority of the divine. And Nala did.

And then came the moment when Nala beheld Damayanti. He found her more beautiful than she had been described to be. Nala had heard of Damayanti's beauty and Damayanti of Nala's charm, but when they saw each other for the first time, their love for each other grew manifold. Nala's mind cautioned him. He was here as a messenger. He had to abide by his promise. Repressing his desires, he gave her the message that celestials would be attending the swayamvara and that she had to choose one from among them. 'But I will choose only you,' said Damayanti.

'Why would you choose a mortal rather than a celestial? Lead your heart to the celestials who are the creators of the world. Even to the dust of their feet I am not equal,' said Nala. He praised each god and described him gloriously. When Damayanti was still not convinced, Nala gave her advice on what was in keeping with the truth, what was in keeping with dharma. That is why Yama recollected this story. Nala told Damayanti, 'Having promised the celestials and having come in their interest, how can I further my own? If virtue could allow one to seek one's own interest, I would gladly do so.'

Damayanti understood. She said, 'Let the celestials and you come to the swayamvara. I will choose according to my desire. No blame will hang on you.'

Nala returned to the celestials, who were eager to know what had transpired. Nala reported everything verbatim, including Damayanti's statement that she wanted to choose him.

The day of the swayamvara arrived. Damayanti went, garland in hand, into the hall where kings, princes and celestials were gathered, waiting with bated breath. When their eyes fell on Damayanti, they rested just where they fell ... for every part of her was so beautiful that no one could wrest their eyes away. As Damayanti walked around the assembly, she saw five persons who were identical in appearance. They all looked like Nala. Damayanti could not identify her Nala. As she peered into the face of each of the five kings, each looked like the real Nala.

With her hands trembling and her lips quivering, Damayanti said, 'I have given my heart to Nala and accepted him as my husband. So that I may abide by Truth, O celestials, assume your forms and point him out to me. I have commenced my worship of King Nala, and so that I abide by Truth, O celestials, point him out to me.'

As Damayanti prayed sincerely thus, she noticed that four of the Nalas had no perspiration on their faces, the flowers in the garlands around their necks were not wilting, and they did not have any sprinkling of dust on them. She noticed that four were also sitting slightly raised from the ground. She had skilfully abided by her dharma, with her sincere and emotional plea, keen observation and complete commitment to Nala. The four celestials too now appreciated her conduct and therefore revealed their original forms. Blessing the couple, they made to depart while Damayanti garlanded Nala. Each of them blessed Nala with a bright future for abiding by his dharma and not succumbing to self-interest. Yama's words to Nala were, 'May you have a refined taste in appreciation of food. May you have the highest place in virtues.'[1]

Yama's blessings were significant, and even today Nala is legendary for having been an excellent chef. The story of Nala is also related every time an example of someone who abided by dharma needs to be given.

Yama sighed. Dharma was not easy to follow. It required a clear mind. And to Yama, Nala stood out as a great example of one who followed dharma. Nala was in love, a handsome, powerful king who was sought after by women, and yet he was a man of great rectitute with his head firmly on his shoulders.

Yama asked the next set of questions of Yudhishthira:

> What is a man's Atman? Who is his friend willed by destiny?
> What is his support in life? What is his refuge?

By Atman, Yama did not mean soul. He meant that which is as close to man as his own soul. Yudhishthira understood what was meant and answered as follows:

> The offspring is a man's dearest, his wife his friend granted by destiny
> Rain supports his life and generosity is his refuge.[2]

28
Yama and Ravana

Now the yaksha seemed very motivated, gesturing to Yudhishthira to sit down if he wished to. But he continued to send questions his way. Yudhishthira remained standing. This time the yaksha told him not to answer his questions after he had asked the first set of four. He asked twelve questions in all, three sets of four, and then leaned back, tapping his clawed fingers on a palm leaf.

> What is the best among that which is highly valued?
> What is the best among wealth?
> What is the best kind of gain? What is the best kind of happiness?
>
> What is the highest dharma in the world? Which aspect of dharma always yields fruits?
> What when followed does not lead people to grieve?
> Association with what never decays?

Renunciation of what makes one more pleasant?
Renunciation of what never leads to misery?
Renunciation of what makes one wealthier?
Renunciation of what makes one happy?

Yudhishthira smiled. He knew why the yaksha had asked these three sets of questions together. They had all to be together. One set pertained to physical and mental attributes. The second to the attitude to be developed and the study which would enable that attitude to build. The third, and in Yudhishthira's opinion, the most important, was about the qualities a seeker should possess in order to make all the attainments referred to in the previous two sets of questions meaningful and lasting. Ravana was a prime example of high learning. He knew the Vedas, had good health, but was neither content nor had renounced his ego, anger, desire or greed.

Yudhishthira replied:

Skill is supreme among that which is highly valued,
learning is the supreme wealth
Good health is the best possible gain and
contentment, the best kind of happiness

Non-violence is the greatest dharma in the world,
study of the three Vedas always yields results

Those who have their mind under control do not
grieve and association with the righteous never
stales

Renouncing the ego makes one more pleasant,
renouncing anger never leads to misery
Renouncing desire makes one wealthier and
renouncing greed makes one happy

Long, long years ago, Ravana, the Dasananan, the ten-headed king of Lanka, was sitting in his palace when Narada visited him.[1] The celestial bard did not always say the right things, but he did instigate the listener. This time Yama was the target. Yama did not know this. Narada began very endearingly, saying to Ravana, 'Listen to me if you wish, O child. Why do you torment the earthly beings? They are already in the grip of death. You, who cannot be destroyed by any, should definitely not trouble the mortals, who are subject to hunger, thirst, old age and hundreds of diseases, doomed as they are by Fate and stand in melancholy and sorrow. In one place there is dance and music going on, in another someone is crying over the dead … let this world and the earthly beings be. If you do want to bring any additional power under your control, attack Yama and subdue him. When he is subdued, everything will be conquered for sure.'

Ravana laughed on hearing this. His laugh was like the rumbling of an autumnal cloud. He liked the idea. 'Then all the three worlds will be under me,' cried Ravana in boisterous glee. Narada assisted him, showing the southward direction along which to proceed for this. 'I will go put an end to Yama who lives in the southern quarter. Think of it as done. My rage is overwhelming me and I will not return till I put that fellow Yama, who torments living beings, to an end,' Dasagriva – another name for Ravana – told Narada.

Narada was, however, taken aback by the intensity of Ravana's resolve as he saw him marching southward with his ministers. 'How will Yama, who controls all three worlds, be subjugated by Ravana? How will Ravana the rakshasa approach of his own accord the exalted king who is brilliant like the sun, is a second fire, who knows the doings of every single being, through whose energy all created beings derive their consciousness, before whom all three worlds recoil in fear? How will Ravana even attempt to conquer the greatest Lord of Justice, Dharma himself?' Curious to witness the encounter and report it as it would take place, Narada also went southward. He was quick paced and reached ahead of Ravana.

There he saw the majestic Yama sitting before the all-knowing fire and meting out justice to earthly beings. He welcomed Narada and offered him due respect and a seat. Gently he asked him how he had come that way, 'O celestial sage! Hope righteousness is not lacking. Hope all is well. What can I do for you?' asked Yama of the mischief-making bard.

Narada replied, 'I have come in a hurry to tell you that the rakshasa Ravana is coming here to subdue you. How will you, the invincible, be conquered? He wishes to conquer you, you who wields the danda for punishment. Please make the necessary preparations.' Even as Narada was speaking they saw a brilliant, star-like light approaching at great speed, and soon the aerial car, Ravana's pushpaka vimana, became visible in all its brilliance, and the rakshasa too came closer.

Ravana had travelled a long distance and seen more than he wished to. He saw Yama's soldiers, along with their assistants, beating and torturing embodied souls. He could hear many screams and wails. He saw many beings being devoured by worms and fierce dogs, he heard painful cries and saw many forced to cross the river Vaitarani, the river of blood, several times. Some others suffering from acute pain were being made to walk on burning sand or a razor's edge. Some were being immersed in sewage water; others were crying of thirst and hunger. Ravana, as his first point of attack, released them all. They were surprised at this unexpected intervention … dazed for a while, they became happy that they were free. Ravana was now nearing Yamapuri, Yama's brilliant city where many blessed souls were enjoying themselves.

But war had begun. Yama's soldiers, shocked that Ravana should release the punished souls, rose in protest. Soon Ravana's ministers and Yama's soldiers were in fierce combat. Even Ravana was engaged in picking up and flinging down soldiers when they approached him. Though his pushpaka vimana was attacked several times, it remained intact as it was by its very nature imperishable. The war became bloodier and bloodier. Yama's soldiers had been taken completely by surprise and were overpowered by Ravana's ministers and by Ravana himself. Hearing the roar of the rakshasas, Yama realised the attacking team was getting the upper hand.

'Get me my chariot,' commanded the Lord of Death, roused as he was to anger.

The huge celestial car and his charioteer stood before him in a trice. With immense energy, the grand lord ascended the chariot with a lance and a mallet in his hands. The one because of whom the world perishes and resurges, the ever-powerful Yama, stood with the kaladanda standing beside him. Nooses hung on all four sides of the chariot. Seeing Yama angry, a rare sight indeed, all the three worlds were fearful of the consequence.

As soon as Yama was in the chariot, the charioteer spurred on the horses, which were very quick in thought and pace. They soon brought Yama the war site. The war turned tumultuous with the two warriors both seeking victory, neither willing to relent. It went on for seven days. Then Ravana shot some arrows that pierced Yama and hurt him. That enraged Yama, his alter ego Kala and all of Yama's men. Then Yama rose like a storm and said, 'Leave him, all of you. I will kill him.' As Yama picked up his kaladanda, flaming with fire, fear spread all around. 'It is time for dissolution,' cried one and all. Ravana's death was now at hand. Then Brahma appeared.

'O! Son of Sun God, O God with immeasurable prowess, surely this rakshasa is not to be killed by you. I have conferred on him a boon that he cannot be killed by a god or a man. If you kill him my boon will be nullified and it will speak very poorly of me. So in order to keep my reputation, this rod cannot be flung,' said Brahma to Yama.

There was a sudden impasse. Was Brahma telling Yama to let the evil Ravana win?

Sometime later, Yama as the yaksha asked Yudhishthira the following four questions:

> What is the sign of penance? What is true restraint?
> What is forgiveness and what is shame?[2]

Yudhishthira answered:

> To be steadfast in one's dharma is penance, to have control over the mind is true restraint
> To live with opposites is forgiveness, and shame is aversion to reprehensible acts.

Yama's response to Brahma's request is described by these answers given by Yudhishthira. Indeed Yama, keeping his faith in Brahma, said, 'If you do not wish it and have granted the rakshasa a boon, then I will respect that, for you are our master. If I am not to fight, what is the point in staying here?' Conquering his mind, Yama walked away from the scene of battle and returned to the heavens with Brahma. Ravana rode back into the world claiming he had defeated Yama, God of Death.

Yama as the yaksha asked another set of questions to Yudhishthira a few minutes later:

> Who is the enemy difficult to conquer? What is the disease that is incurable?
> Who are called honest and who are the dishonest?

Yudhishthira replied:

> Anger is most difficult to conquer, covetousness the incurable disease
> The one who wishes well to all is honest, and the one who is heartless is dishonest.

Yama was very angry with Ravana. But the moment he realised he could not act, he gave up his anger, even though it was righteous indignation. So when Yama asked Yudhishthira these questions, he had the experience and wisdom that framed them.

29

Yama and Harishchandra

Yudhishthira noticed that the yaksha looked a little serious. His body language had become a little sterner. Yudhishthira had begun to feel some affection for the yaksha. Few people could ask such good questions and appreciate his answers. The place the yaksha had chosen to test him was truly scenic. The trees let in golden light, making their leaves appear aquamarine blue. Was it the reflection of the waters of the lake that gave them that colour? Before Yudhishthira could reflect more on that the yaksha called out to him:

> O Rajan (king), tell me what is this world enveloped in? Why is it not able to throw light on or understand many things?
>
> Why do friends fall away and why is it difficult to go to heaven?

Yudhishthira smiled. Was the yaksha being kind to him and making his questions simple?

Ignorance covers the earth and that darkness
obstructs our vision and understanding
Friends are competing for more in greed and so fall
away
And heaven is difficult to get to because of our
attachment to the world.

Yama smiled. His raised his head in a slight nod, seeming to ask if he could go on. Yudhishthira folded his hands in obeisance in response.

Who is dead? Which kingdom is dead?
What renders a shraddha ineffectual and why does a
yajna fail?[1]

Yama's voice was soft as he asked these questions. Yudhishthira replied in the same tone:

A poor person is like a dead one. A kingdom without
a king is a dead one
Lack of a qualified priest renders a shraddha
ineffectual and yajna fails when no cash is given
along with.

The words 'cash is given along with' seemed to resonate in the environs. Whether it was a yajna or a gift in kind, only if cash was given too was the act complete and fulfilled. And the story of only one king came to mind when these words were spoken. It was the story of a king of yore, Harishchandra. A sudden quiet filled the clearing in the forest and both Yama and Yudhishthira seemed lost in reverie. They both seemed to be thinking of Harishchandra. King Harishchandra was turned into a pauper, and his life was as described in Yudhishthira's answer.

Narada, the mischievous celestial bard, had just returned from a visit to the heavens. He was describing the wondrous court of Lord Indra to Yudhishthira. He described the hall and the many great gods and sages assembled there. Yudhishthira, who was listening keenly, asked, 'Why, noble sir, do you mention only Harishchandra among the great kings present there. You take nobody else's name. In what way is he so great that his name is singled out by you?'

Narada described Harishchandra as a very powerful and loved king who was true to his word – to an extent no one before or after was or would be.[2]

Harishchandra was the son of King Trishanku. He ruled well and over a large area. One day he was told that a huge beast was ravaging the crops in his kingdom and the farmers were in grief. Nobody was able to kill or hunt down the beast. The king, compassionate and brave, decided he should set out to hunt down the animal himself, and so he did. As he rode on, he thought he saw the beast here, then there, and soon he was chasing what seemed a mirage. In all the confusion, the king lost his way in the forest. There he heard the voices of women calling out for help. The beast itself had, however, disappeared, leaving the king feeling that it had all been an illusion.

'Save us. Save us please, or we will die,' cried the sweet voices of the maidens, calling out piteously for help. King Harishchandra followed the voices. They seemed to be coming from within a hermitage. Instinctively, he called out, 'Do not worry, I am here to help.' But should he help? How could he enter a hermitage without the hermit's permission? And the hermit was nowhere to be seen. The calls grew more desperate. The king grew greatly concerned. They could be the hermit's wife or daughters calling out to be saved. It was most likely something serious or else their lives would not be in danger. His quickening heartbeat and riotous imagination commanded quick action, and the king barged into the hut. Once within, he saw in the backyard five beautiful maidens trapped among thorny creepers. The more they tried to extricate themselves, the tighter creeper wound around them. 'Save us, save us,' they cried. Harishchandra drew out his sword, and as he was cutting the creeper the maidens wriggled out and flew away!

Dumbfounded, Harishchandra returned to the palace exclaiming, 'Illusions and more illusions and our ignorance!'

As he entered the palace, in stomped Rishi Vishvamitra. On returning to his hermitage, he had been enraged to find the damsels freed and his creepers chopped away. He knew that no one less in stature and courage than King Harishchandra himself could have done this, and so here he was, fretting and fuming. The furious sage was determined to subject Harishchandra to a lot of pain to test his mettle, and so did not limit himself to just handing out a curse.

In a thunderous voice, the sage announced that he had come to seek justice, for someone had freed the five maidens he had held captive. 'Who dared do that?' he roared. In all humility, Harishchandra said he had but done his duty. The duty of a king, he said, was to protect his people, give gifts to brahmins ... and so on.

At this moment both the yaksha and Yudhishthira raised their heads and found themselves looking at each other. Were both thinking the same thoughts, or were these thoughts only in Yudhishthira's head? The yaksha was asking:

What is the reason for gifting brahmins? For gifting performing artistes?
What is the reason for gifting servants? For gifting kings?

Yudhishthira answered immediately:

> To earn religious merit one gifts brahmins, the
> artistes for acquiring fame
> To elicit their support one gifts servants, and kings
> for protection.

Yama was pleased. He too had been thinking of Harishchandra because he, Yama, had played an important role in testing Harishchandra's adherence to Truth.

Vishvamitra asked the king for gifts, and the king was so eager to placate him that he rashly promised the sage anything he should ask for. Vishvamitra seized the opportunity. He asked for all that the king had, the kingdom, the oceans and the land around. The king readily gave him everything. Now the crafty sage said, 'No gift is complete without some cash.'

The king called for a thousand gold coins, only to find Vishvamitra raising his hand. 'You have given me everything … the treasury is no longer yours, Harishchandra. This city, Ayodhya, is also not for you to stay in any longer. Even the clothes you are wearing are mine.'

Then began the saga of Harishchandra. He, his wife, Saivya, and son, Rohitsva, left the palace before sunrise to walk to Kashi. Vishvamitra had insisted the king owed him a thousand gold coins. The king had promised to work and earn it. The sage had given him one month's time.

Bound to honour the promise he had made to the sage, Harishchandra reluctantly sold his wife and son in the slave market. He then continued to stand in the centre of the market square waiting for someone to employ him. No one did. He began wondering how he could earn the other five hundred gold coins he had to give the sage. The stone-hearted sage stood beside him, threateningly. Then came Yama in the guise of a chandala offering to pay him five hundred gold coins if he was ready to cremate dead bodies. The chandala's offer gave Harishchandra the goosebumps. 'No, no, I am a warrior, this is not my job,' said Harishchandra. But Vishvamitra's hand was outstretched, and Harishchandra realised that he was still a warrior but this time the battlefield was his mind. 'I will be your slave instead,' said Harishchandra to Vishvamitra. 'Oh fine, I then order you to work for the chandala,' said Vishvamitra.

Harishchandra knew there was no way out. He followed his new master and worked diligently, crying with every lament of a wife, mother, father, son or daughter. Soon he began looking as unkempt and ash-covered as his master. One night, as a storm raged and darkness gathered itself into the deepest of black, a lone woman walked to the cremation ground with a child in her arms. The sight tore Harishchandra's heart for some reason. He was by now used to sorrow, or so he thought. As she laid down her son and wept, Harishchandra heard himself ask the lady for the fee for the cremation. The lady did not have a penny.

Harishchandra realised the boy was his own son! Were Saivya and Harishchandra to be happy to have found each other, or were they to lament? The night seemed to recoil and nature stood away while Harishchandra arranged the pyre.

How much more were the two to bear? How much longer was Harishchandra to be tested? Even the gods felt they had had enough and soon descended. Yama now threw off his disguise and all the gods assembled to bless the family. Rohitsva sat up and the world sang praise of Harishchandra, the king who kept his word at all costs.

The yaksha looked energised at the way the story ended.

30

Yama and Shibi

The air began to fill with a strange kind of contentment. The yaksha was in no hurry to ask his next question. As he looked around he saw the cranes standing at the edge of the pond. They neither stood deep in the water nor on dry land. That prompted the next set of questions from the yaksha.

He asked Yudhishthira:

Which is the right direction? What is water?
What is food and what is poison?
What is the right time for a funeral ceremony?

Yudhishthira replied:

To follow the righteous is the direction,
The clouds are the source of water
The earth gives us food, greed is poison,
A brahmana is a good time for shraddha
What do you think, O yaksha![1]

The yaksha did not acknowledge Yudhishthira's question. He was still thinking about the cranes, which stood at the edge of the pond, neither in the water nor on land. He wanted to relate to Yudhishthira the story of a king of the future, Vikramaditya, and his encounters with Vetal. Once souls are yanked out of bodies, some of them long for their bodies and are still attached to worldy matters and belongings. They are neither able to and nor wish to cross the river Vaitarani. Vaitarani is a deep river which is not just filthy but hot and teeming with predators. To cross the Vaitarani is the challenge en route to Yamaloka. Vaitarani divides the earthly realms from Yamaloka. Yama thought sadly that such fearful stories had been told in order to compel humans to follow a righteous life. It was said that only the righteous and those for whom a cow had been sacrificed were able to cross this river. The evil fell into it, and their experience was not even worth describing. Yama thought of all this because, like those cranes standing at the edge of the lake, neither in water nor on land, some souls hovered around the cemetery and did not even get to the river. These souls were called pretas, vetals or pishachas. It was believed that they were unable to go forward because the funeral rites, or shraddha, had not been performed for them.

At some level Yama felt all this was meaningless. Every human should strive for knowledge, which would release him and take him straight to Yamaloka. So he asked:

> What is called knowledge? What is tranquillity?
> What is the greatest kindness? What is true simplicity?

Even as Yudhishthira was replying, Yama felt he heard some chaos happening in Yamaloka. He glanced upwards to see, and indeed everyone was searching for him! 'Mahisha is here. So Yamaraja must also be around,' they surmised, and kept looking for him. He was enjoying the commotion as he watched on. He could see many stalwarts – Valmiki, Kanwa, Katyayana and many more such illustrious men. And then he caught sight of King Shibi too, and at the same time he heard Yudhishthira say:

> Knowing Brahman is true knowledge, quiet mind is tranquillity
> Kindness is doing good to all, and equanimity of mind is true simplicity.

How apt, thought Yama. Indeed, this reply described Shibi. The king had been well known for his generosity and kindness. Deciding to test him once, Indra and Agni came into his court. Agni took the form of a dove while Indra followed as a hawk. The dove sought refuge in King Shibi saying, 'A hawk wants to eat me, save me, kind king.' King Shibi promised to do so. Soon the hawk also flew into the court and asked for the dove to be released. 'The dove is my food, you cannot deny me my food,' protested the hawk. In order to feed the hawk and yet save the dove, King Shibi offered his own flesh, which he sliced off from different parts of his body. He fed the hawk till it was satisfied. Watching this, the gods were convinced that this man was kind and generous, and with a mind so stable he did not hesitate to offer himself to save a dove. They restored his body to health and went away satisfied.

King Shibi was now in Yama's assembly hall, singing Yama's praises and enjoying a land which had every object of desire, all kinds of enjoyable articles, including delectable food and drinks, fragrant garlands of every perfume, and was surrounded by trees that would bear fruit as desired. Attending on Yama are all the great kings like Nrga, Yayati, Nahusa, Puru, Vena and Dushyanta, and ascetics like Agastya and Dhruva. They were ascetics of severe penance, of excellent vows and truthful speech, of pure and peaceful minds and of a heart made pure by holy deeds. Interestingly, many kings had the same names, some of the common ones being Dhritarashtra, Bhima, Bhishma and Devraja. There were others who worked for Yama, and yet many more men and women of great repute. All these people attended on Yama with all their heart and sincerity. Apsaras and Gandharvas sang and danced beautifully, and the whole hall was like a place of contentment where wisdom mingled with pleasure.

The wide and expansive hall was exquisitely constructed, so ornate and pleasing that no words could describe it adequately. It is believed that Vishvakarma, the celestial architect, had built it after long years of severe penance.[2]

Yama turned his attention back to Yudhishthira, though his mind was still on King Shibi. He asked him:

> What do sages call steadiness? What do they mean when they say patience?
> What is regarded as the highest ablution? And what is meant by charity?

Yudhishthira answered:

> Steadiness is being rooted in one's dharma
> Controlling one's passions is patience
> True ablution lies in purifying the mind
> To protect all creatures is charity.

As though appreciating the conversation and the thoughts in Yama's mind, a few drops of rain fell. The yaksha became concerned about Yudhishthira getting wet, but it was just a drizzle and soon it stopped.

31
Yama and Rama

The yaksha's voice had now softened. He asked the next question in a deep tone, in a voice as smooth as butter, more meditative and questioning.

> What is it that is termed delusion? What is it that is called pride?
> What is understood by idleness and what is called grief?

Yudhishthira replied:

> Delusion is not knowing one's dharma, pride is a bloated ego
> Failure to perform one's dharma is idleness and ignorance is grief.

Taking a deep breath in, Yama asked the next set of questions:

> What does a person of sweet speech gain?
> What does a person of deliberate action gain?

What does a person with many friends gain?
What does the virtuous gain?

Yudhishthira answered:

A person of sweet speech is loved by all
A person of deliberate action gains more than all
A friendly person lives in happiness
A righteous person gains stature.

Another portrait had been painted in words. Yudhishthira's answer made Yama think of Rama, who was also called Priyamvada, or the one of sweet speech. Yama met Rama under strange circumstances. Brahma had told him to fetch Rama as his time on earth was over. Yama was taken aback. How could he approach Narayana Himself? But he had to do it. And this is how it happened.

Rama had ruled for over ten thousand years. One day, an ascetic appeared at the gate of his palace in Ayodhya. He met the glorious and strong Lakshmana and said, 'Please convey to Rama that I have come here with a very important purpose. I am the messenger of Rishi Atibala, who is very powerful and evolved. I seek to meet Rama.'

Lakshmana was awestruck by this messenger. He immediately went and told his brother, 'A messenger has come who is brilliant as the sun. He wishes to meet you.'

Rama told Lakshmana to let the ascetic in. When he came in it was as though brilliance had taken form. Not only was he glowing from head to toe, but every corner of the room seemed to reflect his brilliance. Rama looked at the ascetic with admiration and respect. The visitor's splendour could not be contained. In a voice as sweet as his presence, he said, 'To your glory, Sri Rama.'

Now, you know the messenger was none other than Yama. Rama and Lakshmana did not know.

Rama, the king, worshipped the ascetic in the right manner, washed his feet, made the right offerings and then asked after his well-being. The ascetic was given a golden seat to sit on, and then Rama said, 'Welcome to you, O wise one, do convey to me the message you carry.'

The attractive messenger cleared his throat and said, 'This message is to be shared only with you by me, no third person can hear it. This is in the best interest of all. Anyone who sees us or hears us, as this message from the great chief is being conveyed from me to you, must be sentenced to death.'

'So be it,' said Rama and told Lakshmana to stand guard outside the door. 'And send away the attendant who normally stands at the door.'

Lakshmana understood what his brother wanted and he quickly went forth to carry out his orders. Rama turned to the ascetic and said, 'Now speak sire, without hesitation. I am eager to hear what you have to say.'

'Listen O King to the great purpose for which I have come,' said the ascetic. 'I have been sent by Brahma who says, "O Lord of the Universe, you had vowed to benefit all the three worlds and that promise has been fulfilled. Prior to creation, you yourself by your Maya, your illusory power, having merged all the worlds in yourself, sleeping on the great ocean, had created me, Brahma. And to me you entrusted the job of creation. I seek your blessings for the protection of the people, for it is from you that I draw my powers. And therefore you have been taking human forms, like that of the Vamana,[1] and now as Rama to kill Ravana, the evil. Your job is now over and your time on earth is also ending. It is time for you to come back to us. If, however, you wish to stay on and protect the people of the earth, please do as you wish, or if you have the desire to protect the gods, return to us."'

Rama smiled gently. Now he knew his visitor was none other than Yama himself. 'I will come, return to the heavens, as Brahma has said,' he said. 'You have spoken what was in my heart, O Yama, to stay with the gods and help them perform their deeds is my wish. I have nothing to ponder over.'

While this conversation was going on behind closed doors, the much-respected Rishi Durvasa came to the palace to meet Rama. Durvasa is known to be of a very hot temper. Even the gods feared his rage. So when he said, 'Lakshmana, lead me to Rama immediately, or else the purpose for which I have come will be lost,' Lakshmana was in a quandary. He gently said, 'What can I do for you, sire? Rama is now a little busy ...' His voice trailed away, his body language was humble. But Durvasa was not one to observe all that. 'It is now or else I will curse this city, Bharata, even Rama and the progeny of everyone in the city ... I am unable to contain my anger any more.'

Now Lakshmana was clear. He reported the arrival of Durvasa to Rama. He knew he would have to die, but if he did not tell Rama the whole city would perish, so it was better for him to die rather than put the people of Ayodhya at risk. That was the logic that made him report the arrival of Durvasa and the sage's desire to meet Rama. Rama hurried out, and after honouring the sage asked what he could do for him. 'I have just finished a thousand years of penance. I want hot food,' said Durvasa.

Rama attended to his request. Durvasa ate, blessed Rama and went away happily. Then Rama saw that Yama had left too. And he realised Lakshmana would have to die. That saddened him very much.

He called his ministers and reported the conversation he had had with Yama. There was deathly silence in his court. Then Vashishta, his principal adviser, hailing the king, said, 'Your end has been foreseen by me, sad though I am to say so. Let him, Lakshmana, go. I have seen your separation from him too. Death is too powerful. Do not give up your promise, for if you do, righteousness will be lost. With righteousness gone, all three worlds will perish.'

Rama gave Lakshmana leave to go, 'Let righteousness not suffer,' he said with a heavy heart. With tears in his eyes Lakshmana walked into the river Sarayu. The gods, led by Indra, came to fetch him. Some days passed, during which Rama made all the necessary administrative arrangements, crowned his sons Luv and Kush as kings of north Kosala and south Kosala and himself declared his job was done. Rama too followed Lakshmana. Of course, his guru, Rishi Vashishta, advised him that since Brahma had sent Yama, he should go. With Lakshmana gone, nothing on earth now interested Rama. He just had to go. His other brothers and many other residents of Ayodhya too followed Rama into the river Sarayu, where Brahma waited on him and Rama emerged as the effulgent Lord Vishnu. As Vishnu, when he went to Vaikuntha, he allotted all those who went with him a heaven named Santanaka.[2]

32

Yama meets his son

Gently, as a father would hold his son's hand and lead him, the yaksha asked:

> Who is a person doomed? Answer quickly this question asked by me.

Yudhishthira replied:

> The one who despite inviting a priest, says he has nothing to give, the one who believes the Vedas and his dharma are false, the miser who does not even donate.

Yama then asked:

> Who is a brahmin?

Yudhishthira replied:

> Hear me O Yaksha! It is neither learning nor birth which determines it. Only good conduct defines a brahmin.

Now, thought the yaksha, he should stop. The king must be really thirsty after having spoken so much. But some questions to emphasise what was required for a good life remained to be asked. The conversation went on thus:

Yama: Who is happy?
Yudhishthira: The one who is not in debt is happy.
Yama: What is it that is amazing?
Yudhishthira: Innumerable people die every minute and yet the remaining live in the dream of immortality.

Yudhishthira smiled. Did the yaksha also have a hint of a smile on his face?

Yama: What is the path?

Yudhishthira:

> Logical discussions are inconclusive
> No one sage's perspective can be taken as the complete Truth
> The principles of Dharma are in hiding
> So following in the footsteps of the great men is the right path.

Yama: What is the great news of the day?

Yudhishthira:

> With earth as the pot, the skies as the lid, the sun as fire, day and nights as fuel and the seasons and months as the stirring ladle, Time is cooking all of us, that is the news.

The yaksha took a little time to climb down from the tree. He now stood on the ground in front of Yudhishthira. But of course, he was still huge, reaching the skies in height, and was very broad too. And as though to sum up the character of the many great people he had been thinking of, Harishchandra in particular, the yaksha said:

> O courageous one, you have answered rightly all my questions
> Now tell me, who is a man? And who is a man richly endowed?

Yudhishthira:

> The one whose praise is sung on earth and the heavens is a man.

'Now,' said the yaksha, 'you have answered all my questions with regard to all that makes a man blessed.

You may therefore choose to bring to life one of your brothers.'

Yudhishthira turned to look at his brothers all sprawled on the ground. Without hesitation he said, 'O Yaksha! Please revive Nakula, the dark one with red eyes and very tall like the sala tree, broad-chested and long-limbed.'

The yaksha laughed a short laugh. 'Why Nakula? He is born of another mother. Bhima is dear to you and Arjuna is your main support. Ask for one of their lives.'

Yuidhishtra was still in question–answer mode.

> The one who gives up dharma gives up himself. I abide by that which is right. I abide by that which is not cruel or violent. One son of Kunti, that is me, is alive, now let one son of Madri, who is equally loved by me, be brought to life.

The yaksha was so delighted with Yudhishthira's answer that he said, 'Let all your brothers be brought to life.'

As the brothers stood up one by one, Yudhishthira now asked the yaksha, 'Who are you? I cannot believe you are a yaksha. You put all these strong men to slumber and now have made them rise from the dead. Who are you?'

Nature held its breath as the yaksha answered, 'I am your father, son. I am Dharma. I came here to see you.'

Overwhelmed with love for his son, Dharma, as Yama introducing himself, said, 'Famed for righteousness, and by the ideals of truth, restraint, purity, simplicity, modesty, steadiness, charity and ascetism, I live. They are like parts of my body. Therefore, it is only through non-violence, an unbiased and impartial outlook, peacefulness, purity, humility that one can access me. You, my son, have done so. You are and have always been dear to me. I am happy to see you are equanimous of mind, exercise control over your mind, are of a forgiving nature and not intoxicated by the senses. I came to test you. Now I am happy, I wish to grant you boons. Ask, O King.'

He transformed back into Yama.

Yudhishthira's eyes opened wide as he saw his father, the bright and brilliant Dharma. He took a deep breath in and his body language changed. He must have been happy to see his father, one presumes. He was, however, very alert and not swayed by emotion; in fact, Yama appeared more sentimental than Yudhishthira did. After such a serious and intense examination, the boon Yudhishthira asked for seemed to belie the seriousness of their conversation. He asked simply, for had he himself not said a steady, equanimous mind is simplicity:

> May the fire sticks of the brahmin carried away by a deer be returned to him.

Remember, the chase for those implements was what had brought the five brothers so deep into the forest. Yudhishthira's father laughed. 'That was me,' he said. 'I took on the guise of the deer so as to drag you into the forest. This boon is granted. Here are the fire sticks and the kindling rod. You may return them to the brahmin. Ask for another boon.'

Yudhishthira was going through tough times, and so the boon he requested was very practical. 'O sire!' he said to his father, 'twelve years have passed in the forest. This is the thirteenth year. May we be able to roam around in the forest without being recognised by any.'

'So be it,' answered Yama. 'No one will recognise you even if do not change your appearance. I also give you five the boon to take on any shape you wish in the thirteenth year of your stay in the forest. Now ask another of me.'

Now Yudhishthira heaved a sigh of relief and looked directly at his father. Finally, he met his eyes and personal contact was made. Folding his hands and bending his head, he said, 'Thank you for giving me a vision of you, O great God of Gods. I have no more boon to ask. My father, whatever you wish to confer on me, I will accept with utmost humility and gratitude. I do, however, seek your blessing that I may never fall into the trap of greed, anger or folly. May my mind always be inclined towards charity, ascetism and truth.'

'You are already blessed with all that, son. But here I grant them again to you.' With a swift caress of Yudhishthira's head, Yama disappeared.

Yudhishthira and his brothers returned the fire sticks and the kindling stick to the grateful brahmin.

33
Yama and Vidura

Yama thought of Vidura as he was returning to his kingdom after meeting Yudhishthira.

There once lived a sage named Mandavya. He was a highly evolved soul, learned, devoted to truth and practising severe ascetism. He sat at the entrance to his hut with his arms raised, observing the vow of silence. And he sat in this manner for many, many years. One day some thieves escaping with stolen treasures passing by saw the sage and an open door and so went in and hid their treasures there. Then they decided they too might as well hide till the soldiers who were chasing them went past. A few moments passed.

The guards who were in pursuit of the thieves soon came running that way. Seeing a sage sitting there they asked him if he knew where the thieves had gone. As the sage was observing the vow of silence he said nothing. One would recall that a similar event had occurred with Rishi Kaushika, who had told the thieves where the people who were fleeing from them were hiding. And Kaushika therefore went to hell. Here the situation was different. The thieves were being chased. They had done wrong. But Rishi Mandavya was not interested in this and other such matters. His eyes were open but his mind was focused on the One and Only.

After questioning him for a while and getting no response, the guards went into the ashram, and on searching for some time found the stolen treasures. They knew the thieves could not be far away and caught them too in time. They now suspected the sage to be hand in glove with the thieves for they were found in his shelter. They took him along with the thieves to the king. The king did not pay attention to the matter except to praise the soldiers for having caught the thieves. They were sentenced to death, as was the punishment of the times. The sage too was included in the punishment. The manner in which death was to come to them was rather painful. They impaled the thieves and the sage on what is called a shula, or stake.

The thieves died by and by, but the sage was in deep meditation and continued to be so. His radiance and the power of his penance were so intense that it drew many ascetics from far and near. They came in the form of birds to see him. With all reverence, they asked to know what had happened. Why should a man of such exaltation be impaled? The sage replied, 'What to say, no one is to blame.' A few days later they heard from the king's guards about what had transpired when the thieves were caught and they told the king of the wrong committed by the guards. The king was very repentant. Seeking forgiveness, he said, 'In ignorance have I made this great mistake. I seek your pardon.' The sage was appeased with the king's apology. The king sought to draw him out of the stake, but he could not do so. The rishi continued to meditate and remained in that state on the stake. He acquired many siddhis, or skills, that ordinary mortals could never aspire to. He became well known on earth. One day he went to the court of Dharmaraja or Yama.

There the sage finally opened his mouth to talk about all that he had gone through and asked Yama, 'What is the sin or offence I have committed to deserve such a punishment? Tell me now, and then witness my ascetic power.'

Yama replied, 'O ascetic! An insect was once pierced by you with a blade of grass. You are suffering punishment for that.'

The sage was shocked. 'You have inflicted a rather harsh punishment on me for a very small act.' The sage cursed Yama saying, 'You will be born on earth in the womb of a low-caste woman. And I establish the rule that henceforth any act committed by anyone before the age of fourteen will not be counted as a sin for the consequences that it may beget. Only if someone is above the age of fourteen will their acts be counted as sins and the consequences of the acts attach to the doer.'[1]

That is how a part of Yama was born as Vidura. Vidura stood out in the milieu he was born in. He was learned in dharma and artha; he was free from avarice and anger; he could see far into the future, was tranquil of mind and always engaged in doing good for the people. His life on earth was much like that of the sage who had been impaled; he lived in an environment of battle and hatred, of evil and muscle power, but he himself lived in dharma. He was very close to his brothers, Dhritarashtra and Pandu. He was good in all aspects of learning. His wisdom was like an unmanifested crown on his head and his advice was valued all through the fight between the Pandavas and the Kauravas.

When the battle between the Kauravas and the Pandavas ended, with the Pandavas winning, Dhritarashtra, his wife, Gandhari, Kunti and Vidura left for the forest. They lived there for nearly six years. The Pandavas were not comfortable with this separation, and they went to the forest to meet them. Yudhishthira was upset to find Vidura was not with them. When he asked about Vidura he was told that he had given up all desires and was wandering in the forest. The next morning, when Yudhishthira was going for his bath to the river Ganga, he saw Vidura there, sitting still in deep meditation. He did not respond to Yudhishthira, but the moment he was told Yudhishthira had come he gave up his life. He merged with Yama and returned to the heavens. Yudhishthira performed his last rites, as he was the son of Yama and Vidura was Yama himself.[2]

The thought of his life as Vidura had made Yama pensive. Breaking his reverie was a crow cawing away. That made Yama break into a smile. He looked at it, acknowledged it. The crow was delighted. It cawed even more. Once there had been a king called Marutta. He was performing a sacrifice and all the gods were in attendance. An evolved sage, a knower of dharma, by the name of Samvrata, was conducting the sacrifice. At that time, as luck would have it, Ravana was flying past. He was creating havoc everywhere he went, and as Yama had got to know even earlier, the boon Ravana had secured from Brahma had made him very arrogant. Even the gods were reluctant to face him, for they knew Brahma would never allow them to kill Ravana. When they saw Ravana, all the gods present, Indra, Kubera, Varuna and Yama, were worried. Indra went and hid in the body of a peacock. Kubera hid in a chameleon.

Varuna hid within a swan, and Yama chose a crow that was perched on a tree.

When Ravana descended, Marutta went up to him and asked who he was. Ravana laughed out aloud and told him he was one who was vanquishing the entire world. Thereafter the grand rakshasa, with his imposing and frightening personality, went on to introduce himself as the half-brother of Kubera by the name of Ravana.

King Marutta was no less spirited. 'You conquered your own elder brother, then you must truly be brave,' said Marutta derisively. 'You must indeed be great to have got so many boons, and I know of no other such person. However, I do know that you are not going back alive from here.'

As Marutta drew his sword for a combat, Rishi Samvrata came running to stop him. 'You are in the process of performing a yajna. If you do not finish it, your entire race will be destroyed. And if you indulge in fighting while you are performing the yajna, you cannot continue to perform it. So stop right now.'

King Marutta heard his preceptor with humility and dropped his sword immediately. He tried to block the sound as Ravana continued laughing so loudly that all three worlds could hear him. Ravana left, but not before devouring some sages who had come for the yajna.

Ah! When he left, everyone and everything relaxed, be it a plant or even an inert plate. The gods who were in hiding emerged from their respective hideouts. Indra gave the peacock the boon of colourful feathers. Kubera stroked the chameleon as he emerged out of it and said, 'Your head will be of a golden hue.' Varuna gave the swan her body colour of white and said, 'Like the moon the very sight of you will bring great joy.'

When Yama emerged out of the crow, it flew and sat on the shed constructed for the sacrifice until the yajna ended. Yama said to the crow, 'O bird, I am very pleased with you, now listen to my words which come from a deep sense of gratitude towards you. Since I am pleased with you, rest assured, you will not be affected by the many diseases and ailments that plague all living beings. Further, dear bird, you do not have to fear Death. You will live long, unless people kill you.' Yama added a few words thereafter, which echo in the world up to this day, and people too make sure that no one kills a crow. Yama said, 'When people feed you, all those who are travelling to or are in Yamaloka will feel their hunger is satiated.'[3] That is why even today people feed crows every morning before they sit down to eat themselves. Even during funeral ceremonies and shraddhas, feeding crows is equal to sending food to our ancestors in Yamaloka.

Once the gods had granted their blessings to the animals that had given them shelter when Ravana was around, they returned to their heavenly abodes.

Yama was back in Yamapuri. Amid many cries like, 'Here he is, here he is, he is back,' and 'Where had you gone? Mahisha was still here,' Yama entered his mansion, taking long strides. He was both satisfied and tired.

Book 7

THE ONE AND ONLY

34

The most feared king

Chitragupta, the mind-born son of Brahma, was Yama's close aide. When Yama's role changed from that of a guide to the netherworld to one who sits in judgement on the actions of mortals, he felt the desperate need for an assistant to maintain a log book for each and every life on earth. People are not to be judged only by their physical acts; their mental inclinations and intentions should also be factored in to complete the picture. How was Yama to keep track of so many beings all by himself? Brahma meditated on the problem for a while. From his body sprang Chitragupta, aptly called so. Chitragupta can be translated to mean 'hidden picture'. He was to be the hidden hand behind all of Yama's decisions. He, dedicated as he was to his job even as he emerged into being, came carrying with him an inkpot and a pen. Some say he had a palm leaf also in one of his hands. The collection of palm leaves on which he calculated the debits and credits that accrued to each individual on the basis of his or her actions, thoughts and deeds, is a log book of sorts and is called *Agrasandhini*.

Chitragupta lived in Yamapuri. In time he married one of Yama's daughters, Iravati, and one of Yama's brother Manu's daughters, Nandini.

One afternoon, when all was calm and quiet in Samyamanapuri, Chitragupta was sitting in the presence of Yama. They had finished their conversation on work-related matters. Then Chitragupta commented, 'Sire, will you be meeting someone like Nachiketas or Savitri later in the day today?'

Yama laughed. 'No, Chitragupta,' said Yama. 'On earth much time has passed since I met them. For us one day of Brahma makes a full day. So I met them only this morning. Within our one day, the mortals live a thousand cycles of four yugas. This cycle the mortals are in currently began with Krita Yuga when everything was perfect. Then came the Treta Yuga in which sacrifices were introduced and virtue decreased by a quarter. Truth, which was man's nature, became a practice, that is, a cultivated trait, and men devoted themselves to religion and religious rites. In the Dvapara Yuga virtue decreased by half and the Vedas became divided into four parts. Fewer people devoted themselves to truth. In the Kali Yuga, in which the mortals are now, only one quarter of virtue remains. Truth falls into disuse and the nature of creatures degenerates. Diseases, lassitude, anger, deformities, natural calamities, anguish and fear of famine take possession of the world. That does not mean there are no righteous people. There are still those who are the embodiment of penance like Savitri and there are those who are thirsty to discover the Ultimate like Nachiketas – I just have not interacted with them.'

Chitragupta nodded gravely. 'I am experiencing the impact of the Kali Yuga on earth,' he said, spreading out his arms to show the hectic activity in the suburbs of Yamapuri. Both Chitragupta and Yama laughed. 'Yes,' said Yama, 'this is indeed the impact of the Kali Yuga.'

Construction activity was on the rise. At one end of the great city, measuring a thousand yojanas and laid out as a square, was Chitragupta's residence. It was a sprawling residence with beautiful gardens and tall ramparts embedded with precious stones. Everything about the house was majestic, grand and beautiful. Chitragupta sat on a grand and ornate throne, exuding power as he prepared balance sheets all round the year. He was generally a quiet being but so powerful was he that all over the mortal world there are temples dedicated to him.

Around Chitragupta's house, it is said, are many cottages. To the east is the great house of fever. That establishment takes care of those dying of fever. To the west are houses of dyspepsia, biliousness and other gut-related problems. To the north is the house of jaundice and consumption. To the northwest is the house of headaches.[1] Now many more were being added.

The house of consumption used to be very full some centuries ago, now it was less populated and it began to also be the house of myalgia. A new cottage was constructed for the aged, nowadays many people were dying just of old age. So Chitragupta had to attend to that task too – making provisions for all the newer causes of death.

Continuing the conversation, Chitragupta said, 'One large house of fear would have been, administratively speaking, an easier idea. Most people, in Kali Yuga die of fear rather than any disease itself.' Yama was delighted with Chitragupta's suggestion and told him a story set in present times in the world.

'One day I was riding my brown horse and passing through the region known as China when a philosopher of those times, Confucius, saw me. "Where are you going?" Confucius asked me. "Just to pick up those fallen to plague," I replied. "How many are they?" asked Confucius. "About five hundred," I replied. "Don't pick up more than five hundred," said Confucius to me, implying that I should spare the others. I nodded cheerfully and said, "I will not."

'A few days later we met again. This time I was on my way back here. "So," asked Confucius, "what is the number? Hope you have not exceeded five hundred."

'I laughed. "Look, it is no fault of mine. I went to take five hundred souls, another four thousand five hundred died out of fear. I had no role to play ..."

'Confucius looked sternly at me, but in a split second realised that what I was saying was true. That is why I say that the apt phrase describing Kali Yuga is, "The one who fears dies".

'Why do mortals fear me so much?' wondered Yama. 'Is it not natural that matter decays and deteriorates? The body seems to succumb to disintegration. The mind revolts. The mind is frightened. So much so that death is a shunned topic, no one speaks about death or Yama. It isn't a daily conversation, it is something to be avoided, something that is inevitable but to be kept as far away as possible. To really and deeply appreciate the immensity, the vastness, the grandeur or the vitality of death, there needs to be freedom from fear.'

If you reflect on it, it is true that from the day that you start to think, you begin preparing for death. Consciously or unconsciously. Those who do not are branded foolish, like Amrita. A man named Amrita had an insurmountable fear of death, and he practised many austerities in order to avoid death. Yama was pleased with him and so appeared before him. 'Only those who are about to die or are dead can see me, but pleased with your penance, I am granting you my vision,' said Yama to Amrita.

Amrita bowed before the Lord of Death and said, 'If I have to die anyway, if death is inevitable, can you give me advance notice? Then I will prepare myself. I will ensure my family is comfortable and observe such austerities that in my next birth I am fit to be an ardent worshipper of Krishna.'

Yama granted him his wish. 'I will send you messages,' said Yama.

That gave Amrita great reassurance. He lived happily thereafter, feeling assuaged that he would not die suddenly one morning. As time wore on, whenever he looked at himself in the mirror, he saw one more hair turned grey. He pretended he did not notice. So what if his hair was grey? His life was long, Yama had not contacted him yet.

Then the local elders approached him. In old age, one should turn towards God, they said, and invited him to join in spiritual activities. 'Not now,' said Amrita, 'I still have many more years to enjoy.'

Some more years passed. By this time Amrita had lost most of his teeth. 'Now,' said those devotees of the Lord, 'it is definitely time to turn to God.' Amrita refused. 'Yama has not come to tell me my time is coming to a close,' thought Amrita.

In a few years Amrita's eyesight became weak. But Amrita was still engaged in the material world. His back became bent and his legs weak. But he still felt life would be endless.

Finally, one day, Yama appeared. 'Come on,' he said.

'Where to?' asked Amrita. 'You have not given me time.'

'Your body was constantly telling you and good people advising you, but you refused to take heed.' Amrita started to cry, his mind seized with fear.

The end had come and he had ignored all the signs. That, reflected Yama, was the way all mortals lived, believing in the feeling of everlasting continuity of the body, fearing death.

Chitragupta was still in Yama's presence. 'Let me tell you more about the present times,' said Yama. 'There are still people who think about death and life and how to prepare for it.'

Yama told Chitragupta about a child born in Madanapalle who would grow up to be a renowned philosopher. His name was Jiddu Krishnamurti. Since time is calculated in terms of the English calendar in the mortal world, Yama strained to fit his recollection into a time slot so that earth dwellers could understand. For Yama and Chitragupta it was still the afternoon of the same day. Jiddu Krishnamurti was born in 1896, Vikram Samvat 1953.

About fear of death, Jiddu Krishnamurti had said: 'Fear of losing a loved one, fear of losing the property, the learning, all that which has been acquired in one's lifetime. All the thoughts make up our consciousness. If these are lost then the content of my consciousness is lost. So, can the content of consciousness be totally emptied? When the content is totally emptied, that means no attachment.'

Yama wanted to clarify that it is not a severe, cold, unfriendly detachment that is implied but an understanding of attachment, dependency, acquisition, power, position, anxiety and all that. The emptying of that is real death.

The consciousness on an average creates its own limitations, its own frontiers. When the consciousness is empty, has no clutter, every moment is a new beginning and a new end. Yama smiled as he thought of how Krishnamurti made an important distinction when he said, 'So, death comes to the living when the content of consciousness which makes its own frontier, its own limitation, comes to an end. Along with its unconscious content.'

That was the crucial distinction: 'unconscious content'. It is easy to understand man's attachment to his house, property, spouse, parents, learning, etc., but Krishnamurti said there is more beneath all this, and that is the 'unconscious content'. According to him this unconscious content is a 'deeper content', by which he meant all the prejudices and categories we have formed in our minds over our several births. These categories, these classifications may not have been consciously formed. Even without our knowing, they exist in our minds. To empty the mind of these notions is not easy because our very identity is then at stake. I define myself as erudite or strong … if I have to give up that thought, if I have to empty my mind of that idea, then who am I? Where am I? Am I being completely negated? Why did I work all my life to build myself if I have to give up the idea of being something, a businessman, an athelete, a writer? The idea of being lost in this vast universe without an image for myself brings great anxiety and fear. It is like losing myself. In order to save myself I crave to immortalise myself.

'I am the leveller,' thought Yama. Whatever learning or power and pelf a mortal may have, he or she still has to die, and when cremated, everyone's ashes look similar. It may sound crude, thought Yama, but that was the truth, and he recited to himself a verse:

> There is no armour against Fate;
> Death lays his icy hand on kings:
> Sceptre and Crown
> Must tumble down,
> And in the dust be equal made
> With the poor crookèd scythe and spade.[2]

At this point Yama recollected Yajnavalkya. Yajnavalkya was a great saint and thinker. Yama remembered Yajnavalkya not in the context of the answer to the question as to why there is fear but about what it means to 'empty the consciousness'. And there is an interesting story to this.

One day the great sage Yajnavalkya called both his wives, Katyayani and Maitreyi, and told them he wanted to give up his life as a householder and move into the fourth stage, the stage of vanaprastha, when after having given up all worldly pursuits he would engage in meditation of the Eternal alone. To that end he wanted to distribute his property between his two wives. Maitreyi was amused that her spiritually evolved husband should make such an offer to her. 'If one could make believe that she was the owner of the entire earth, would she find happiness?' she asked him. Yajnavalkya answered her in the negative, saying she would be comfortable but still would not be able to buy immortality with wealth. So Maitreyi replied as Nachiketas had, 'Then what is the good of all this? If one day death is to swallow me up, and transiency is to overwhelm me, the impermanence of the world is to threaten me, what good can accrue to me from this that you are bestowing upon me, as if it is of great value? What am I to do with that thing which is not going to make me perpetually happy, immortal, satisfied?'

Then Yajnavalkya explained to his wives a great secret to immortality: when knowledge is not linked to an object, when the known is the knower and the knowledge, when knowing exists only of the Self.[3]

Yama thought of the human being's long struggle to immortalise himself. It is a good struggle, he reflected. Great works of creativity have emerged out of the desire among human beings to immortalise themselves. A work of art or literature may disappear with time or by accident or even wanton destruction, but the beauty that it inspires will remain forever – that is the immortal element in any creation. A simple thought came into Yama's mind: look at a flower, it blooms and wilts. But the beauty it radiates, its fragrance, its colours, remain in the memory of the earth. The feeling of being bereft of beauty is death. Brahman is Satyam Sivam Sundaram, reflected Yama … living daily in beauty, be it in thought or action, is to come as close to Brahman as possible. Like the beautiful sentiment that arose in Garuda when he saw a little bird, which was also beautiful.

Once, all the gods were travelling to Mount Kailasha to meet Siva. So was Yama. Upon reaching there Yama saw Garuda at the gate and understood that Garuda, the vehicle of Vishnu, had just dropped off his master there. He smiled at Garuda. He also saw a beautiful little bird perched on the branch of a tree by the gate. Yama went in.

Meanwhile Garuda, who had been following every movement of Yama's with a view to understanding what this most feared king would do next, caught him looking at the bird. 'Oh! Yama looked at the bird, that means the bird's days are numbered. Such a beautiful bird, I must save the bird,' thought Garuda, and flew into an obsessive panic. He quickly took the bird and flew as far away as he could, across many seas, and finally landed near a lake in the Dandakaranya forest, where he dropped off the bird. He returned just as the gods were leaving after meeting Siva. Luckily, Yama came out before Vishnu did, and so Garuda had the opportunity to watch him and his reaction when he saw the bird was gone. With a smug expression on his face, Garuda caught Yama looking in the direction of the branch where the bird had been sitting. 'Sire,' said Garuda respectfully, with a little curiosity and a small sense of accomplishment, 'are you looking for the bird you saw here before you went in? Why had you noted it before going in?'

'Oh that?' smiled Yama, and Garuda felt that maybe he was not so fearsome after all. Yama continued, 'When I chanced to see that lovely bird, I saw that it was going to be swallowed by a python in the Dandakaranya forest, near a lake. I wondered how that could happen because its moment of departure from the world was almost here. And the bird was so small. How could its wings take it to the Dandakaranya forest which is so far away?' There was a moment's silence. Garuda felt his vison was getting hazy. He had been so foolish. He, not Yama, had taken the bird to its death. Yama was speaking again, softly. 'But something must have happened …' he mused as he drove away on Mahisha.

Garuda had still not recovered. He heard what Yama said with his mouth agape. Did Yama know it was he who had played into the hands of fate?

Yama hoped Garuda now understood that he, Yama, was just doing his duty as one who transported those souls whose life on earth had been completed to their resting place before they returned to earth again. This samsara is a cycle. But the incident remained in his memory because of the beauty of the bird, because of the beauty of Garuda's sentiment towards it.

35
Yama meets Ramana

Chitragupta was standing before his master Yama, who seemed lost in his thoughts. Chitragupta bowed and cleared his throat, seeking permission to leave his presence. Yama guffawed. Chitragupta was always so serious! He wanted to chat with him.

'Can I tell you about that fearless man?' Yama asked Chitragupta.

'Of course,' replied Chitragupta in all humility, and added, 'sire, we both were there together at his father's funeral ceremony.'

Yama laughed again. Chitragupta was asking him what was new in what he was telling him! So Yama waved aside the idea of telling him the story and gave permission to Chitragupta to go back to his abode.

Yama remembered that the fearless man's father's name was Sundaram Iyer. Sundaram Iyer was married to a lady called Azhagammal. They lived in Thiruchuzhi, Virudhunagar, Madras Presidency, as it was called in the latter part of the nineteenth century CE. They had four children – Nagaswami, Venkataraman, Nagasundaram and a daughter called Alamelu. Nagaswami and Venkataraman were two years apart. Then, after a gap of seven years, came Nagasundaram, and Alamelu, a year later. Theirs was a normal, typical south Indian family, pious and hardworking. Sundaram Iyer was a court pleader. So it was no wonder that when Venkataraman was about six years old, he was caught playing with an old disposed case bundle of lawsuits. He was making kites and boats from the paper.

Very soon things changed. Yama still remembered the date: it was 18 February 1892. Sundaram Iyer's time on earth was over. Yama had also gone, without anyone knowing it, and was watching as his messengers, the yamadhutas, did their job. As he was taking in the area and environs, he saw Venkataraman standing in a corner of the room where the body of Sundaram Iyer lay. Everyone was weeping. Sundaram Iyer was only forty-two years old. His family was still young. There was sorrow. Yama observed that Venkataraman alone had a strange, quizzical expression on his face. He heard him say, 'Why is everyone saying father has gone? He is lying there.' Then someone said, 'If this is your father he would talk to you, smile and do such things. Now you see he is just lying there, he is not responding to you. He is dead.'

Yama watched the twelve-year-old child become pensive. He could read the child's mind. Venkataraman was thinking to himself, 'All this while I was thinking this body to be my father. But now they say my father has gone. And this body is obviously not my father … then what is the difference between the body lying there and my own?'

Yama moved closer to the child, unseen. He involuntarily wanted to comfort the child. And that happened. After thinking a little while, Venkataraman told himself, 'I know that *I* am in my body, but the *I* in my father's body has gone.'[1]

A profound realisation in a twelve-year boy went almost unnoticed.

When all the funerary rites were concluded, Venkataraman went back to school.

He had begun his schooling in Thiruchuzhi, where he had attended a local school. His father wanted him to study in an English-medium Hindu school so that he would be eligible to join government service. It was therefore decided to send Venkataraman, then eleven years old, and his elder brother Nagaswami to their maternal uncle in Dindigul, to stay with him and study there. When his father passed away, a year later, he came back to Thiruchuzhi. In the meanwhile, his uncle got posted to Madurai, and Nagaswami and

Venkataraman were sent to live with him in Madurai to pursue their schooling. They went to the American Mission High School.

Venkataraman was not a very motivated student. History, maths and science did not capture his attention. He had a phenomenal memory but did not seem to use it for his studies. But early in his teens he is said to have been able to correct his Tamil teacher. He had an intuitive grasp of the language. He was, however, physically fit. He stood foremost in sports like swimming, wrestling, staff fighting and football. He also had an extraordinary amount of luck – so much so that every team wanted him when they were playing team sports like football. He therefore came to be called 'Thangakai', or 'golden hand', symbolising how lucky he was.

The uncle's house was a modest two-storeyed structure. It was about a kilometre's distance from the Meenakshi temple in Madurai. Venkataraman was not overly religious, but perhaps had a genetic disposition to spirituality. One of his father's brothers and his father's paternal uncle had become renunciates. Between the ages of twelve and sixteen, Venkataraman happened to read the *Periyapuranam*, the canonical account of the sixty-three Saiva Nayanars, written by Sekkilar, a twelfth-century Tamil saint-scholar. 'Oh!' he thought, 'so union with the divine does happen.' He had heard the name of Arunachala, but never realised it was a mountain very close to Madurai.

When someone returned from there and told him so, he was surprised. 'Ah! It is not a mythical place,' he exclaimed to himself. So many ideas and places that he had thought belonged in the realm of imagination were now turning out to be real places.

Yama somehow took a liking to this child, and whenever he passed by, he would stop to see how he was doing. Sometimes he came just to see Venkataraman. He would watch him from a distance and go away.

One afternoon, Venkataraman was sitting alone on the first floor of his uncle's house. In his words:

> It was about six weeks before I left Madurai for good that the great change in my life took place. It was quite sudden. I was sitting alone in a room on the first floor of my uncle's house.[2]

Yama, as usual, peeped in. He saw Venkataraman alone. What was it about him that Yama liked? He, Yama, knew Venkataraman's past lives. He knew he was a very evolved soul. That is why when Venkataraman's friends marvelled at his memory, Yama just smiled. Venkataraman could grasp and remember everything he read.

Another trait he exhibited was that when he slept, he went into very deep sleep and could not be woken up easily. Sometimes he found he was sleeping in a place different from the one where he had lain down!

But above all, Yama knew Venkataraman had cracked the secret of life as he had watched his father lying lifeless. The crucial discovery was, 'I know that *I* am in my body, but the *I* in my father's body has gone.' Yama wanted Venkataraman to think about this realisation of his just a little more, for therein lay the essence of the cycle of life and death.

Thinking such thoughts, Yama edged closer to catch a glimpse of Venkataraman's face. But suddenly, Yama had gone too close and Venkataraman became aware of his presence!

> I seldom had any sickness, and on that day there was nothing wrong with my health, but a sudden violent fear of death overtook me.

Actually, it was Yama who got scared, frightened. 'Oh no! This boy has sensed my presence!'

Venkataraman did experience fear at the thought of death, but he was voluntarily entering into an experience of death, without fear. He, like Nachiketas, wanted to know what death meant. Yama was embarrassed that Venkataraman had felt his presence. Yama hurriedly took a step back. He had not planned to make his presence felt to Venkataraman. But Venkataraman was a very sensitive and evolved soul, so had perceived Yama's presence – like Rishi Gautama, who had observed penance for sixty thousand years on Mount Pariyatra and therefore had become sensitive to the presence of Yama when Yama had gone to see him. This was a boy of just sixteen, and he had been able to sense him, Yama, in his room. Yama panicked, wondering how to leave without upsetting the young lad.

Meanwhile Venkataraman was thinking:

> There was nothing in my state of health to account for it, and I did not try to account for it or to find out whether there was any reason for fear. I just felt, 'I am going to die,' and began thinking what to do about it.

'You are not, Venkataraman, you have many more years to live,' Yama wanted to say. He had just wanted to be an observer. But now, when he saw Venkataraman say, 'I am going to die,' Yama felt like introducing himself. This moment was not like any other. A fearless human was reaching out to face death, to meet Yama, consciously and with equanimity. Few were prepared to meet death; generally, they tried to escape when the time came. But this boy wanted an encounter with Death. And Yama felt like appearing before him. Not as Yama, as when he had met Savitri, not as Mrtyu as when he had met Nachiketas, not as Kala as when he had met Markandeya and not even as Dharma as when he had met Yudhishthira. He wanted to meet Venkataraman as Vaivaswata, the effulgent son of Surya, the sustainer of the world. He wanted Venkataraman to get the energy of the Undivided, the One.

'Do not fear me,' Yama communicated to Venkataraman. 'I am the eternal YOU. When the muck created by thoughts is cleaned out, this is what remains in you, just the Eternal.' He wanted to tell Venkataraman what he had told Nachiketas:

> The sense objects are higher than the senses
> The mind is higher than the sense objects
> The intellect is higher than the mind
> And the expansive Soul is higher than the intellect.
>
> The unmanifest is higher than the expansive soul
> The purusha (person) is higher that the unmanifest
> And higher than the purusha, there is nothing at all
> That is the end, He is the goal
>
> Hidden as He is in every being
> Invisible he is for appearances
> The wise ones who can see the subtle
> Spot Him with their refined focus and fine perception[3]

But Yama was not speaking with Venkataraman. He was just allowing him to experience the eternal.

Yama saw that Venkataraman was continuing to think:

> It did not occur to me to consult a doctor, or my elders or friends; I felt that I had to solve the problem myself, there and then.

Yama was touched. One of the most important lessons to learn is that one is born alone and dies alone. The journey to the earth and back to Yamapuri has to be undertaken alone. To seek the strength for this within oneself is the greatest tool for any spiritual growth. Venkataraman was going on:

> The shock of the fear of death drove my mind inwards and I said to myself mentally, without actually framing the words, 'Now death has come, what does it mean?'

Yama laughed. Since he became the king of the netherworld, this question had plagued mankind, beginning with Yami. Yama felt like saying, 'Venkataraman, the answer depends on whom you are asking the question to. If you ask a doctor, the doctor will probably say that death is the irreversible end of life, when the vital organs stop working and the body can no longer sustain itself. Death is the permanent cessation of all vital functions, such as breathing, heartbeat and brain activity.

'If you ask a philosopher, he or she may say that to be dead is a state of mind. When you are no longer able to participate in meaningful activities you are dead.

'If you ask a Vedantin, he or she would tell you death is part of the world of changes where the soul goes through the cycle of birth and death in the three worlds. Vishnu Himself is said to have told Garuda:

> In the last moment, Vainateya
> A divine vision arises
> And all three worlds appear as one ...
> As the worn-out senses are finally destroyed
> As intelligence gets foggy
> The messengers of Yama come nearby
> And life departs
> When the breath leaves its place
> The moment of dying seems endless
> And the sensation is like that
> Of the sting of a hundred scorpions[4]

'If, however, one was to ask Swami Vivekananda, the answer would be of another order. One of his disciples, Mrs Bull, had lost her father and was in grief. Swamiji comforted her in his letter to her saying, "Coming and going is all pure delusion. The soul never comes nor goes. Where is the place to which it shall go, when all space is in the soul? When shall be the time for entering and departing, when all time is in the soul? The earth moves, causing the illusion of the movement of the sun; but the sun does not move. So Prakriti, or Maya, or Nature, is moving, changing, unfolding veil after veil, turning over leaf after leaf of this grand book while the witnessing soul drinks in knowledge, unmoved, unchanged. All souls that ever have been, are, or shall be, are all in the present tense … We are in them. They are in us … The whole secret is, then, that your father has given up the old garment he was wearing and is standing where he was through all eternity …"

'Sometime later, Swami Vivekananda spoke on death again, saying, "Death overtakes everything which is complex. The soul is a single element, not composed of anything else, and therefore it cannot die. By its very nature the soul must be immortal. Body, mind and soul turn upon the wheel of law – none can escape. No more can we transcend the law than can the stars, than can the sun – it is all a universe of law. God is the only one who is free. God and freedom are one and the same."'

As though reading Yama's mind, Venkataraman was now answering the question:

> What is it that is dying? The body dies. And I at once dramatized the occurrence of death. I lay with my

limbs stretched out stiff as though rigor mortis had set in and imitated a corpse so as to get greater reality to the enquiry.

Yama recollected Parikshit, just to tell Venkataraman in a light-hearted manner that he could take people whether they were standing, sitting, in hiding or having a meal. Venkataraman did not have to lie down to simulate death. Death or Yama lives in every cell of the body, whatever the posture. But Venkataraman was discovering more profound things, so Yama decided not to dwell on the story of Parikshit just then.

When Parikshit, the Kuru king, had been cursed to die of a snakebite, he took great care to live in a secluded place where there were no snakes. Then Yama instructed his messengers to enter the palace with fruits that had worms in them and travel into Parikshit's apartments. When the king took a bite of a fruit, he died instantly.

Death does not need a specific posture or preparation. When it comes, it happens. But shavasana, or the posture that Venkataraman had assumed, is not one that comes without any preparation. It is also called mrtasana, or the posture of a corpse. Venkataraman not only slipped into that asana, he also stopped breathing. He held his breath within.

Venkataraman's mind was preparing for death; there was no fear, no hesitation. He was thinking that now that Death had come, he would receive him fully. He would prepare himself to host him. So Venkataraman lay down and surrendered himself to experience death.

36

Ramana experiences Yama

> I held my breath and kept my lips tightly closed so that no sound could escape, so that neither the word 'I' nor any other word could be uttered.

Venkataraman was very close to Yama. Yama could feel Venkataraman's breath being drawn in sharply. The seriousness of the boy made Yama want to embrace him. Oh no! he shrank back. That would be not be right. He could not take Venkataraman away ahead of time. Venkataraman focused and concentrated deeply. Yama knew he would have to leave the room soon, but he decided he would let Venkataraman have a glimpse of him, of his effulgent self. Of Vaivaswata.

Venkataraman's body was inert and stiff.

> 'Well then,' I said to myself, 'this body is dead. It will be carried stiff to the burning ground and there burnt and reduced to ashes.' But, with the death of the body, am I dead? Is the body 'I'?

Yama was overwhelmed. This young boy had made out the difference between body and soul. He had found the key. Even King Trishanku had not been able to understand this. King Trishanku ruled over Ayodhya and was a pious and good king. His only problem was that he was overtly attached to his body. He wanted to go to heaven with his body. All the sages, particularly Rishi Vashishta, who was his spiritual adviser in court, refused to help him ascend to the heavens with his body. But Vishwamitra promised to help. He sent Trishanku up to the heavens with his body. As the king was rising up in the air, King Indra saw him and sent him back. Vishwamitra was furious. 'Stop, stop,' he cried, and Trishanku stopped midway, with his head down. There he remains to this day. It is another matter that the constellation of the Great Bear was created for Trishanku's well-being. But he is neither on earth nor in the heavens. To experience the bodyless state is to experience that which lies beyond the physical body. While Yama yanks the spirit away, Agni reduces the body to ashes.

A silence enveloped the room. The calls of street vendors, the bells clanging in the Madurai Meenakshi temple, the cows mooing … everything stopped. There was nothing in the air and yet it was full. Yama embraced the young man for a fraction of a second. A brilliance unable to be contained burst forth …

> It is silent and inert but now there is still something existing and shining! Then this perishable body is not me. I and it are different. I am the indestructible 'I' (Self). Of all things, That Self, unbound by the body, alone is real. The body dies but the Spirit that transcends it cannot be touched by death. That means I am the deathless Spirit.
>
> All this was not dull thought, it flashed through me vividly as living truth which I perceived directly, almost without thought process.

The vast and profound silence now just wrapped Venkataraman in its embrace. So he later said, 'Take refuge in silence. You can be here or there or anywhere. Fixed in silence, established in the inner "I", you can be as you are …'

A complete stillness filled the air. Not even the breath moved. In that state, for that amount of time, not even for as long as it takes for the eyelid to blink, Venkataraman beheld Vaivaswata. That is why it was like a vivid flash. In that split second, his soul was one with the divine. Though his body was inert, his being was illuminated. He had experienced true knowledge. It was a direct experience. No mortal had till then entered the realm of immortality and returned to the mortal world. Venkataraman had. The brilliance seemed to say as it were, 'Shine forth this brilliance to the world.' Thus was born Ramana Maharishi from Venkataraman.

Ramana found that the fear of death, which had risen in him, vanished once and for all. He had instead unravelled the secret of life. The encounter he had just had with the Supreme, the knowledge that he was nothing else but that Supreme, brought about a realisation that stayed with him for the rest of his life. The self-realised state became his natural state, 'unbound by time and space and without increase or decrease'. In a beautiful moment, in complete silence, Venkataraman had attained Self Knowledge. And that changed his life forever.

Yama left. In an instant everything returned to as it was before. The lady outside was selling spinach. The temple bells were ringing, the cyclist was sounding the bell ... what had happened in between?

Years later, when Venkataraman was recollecting this experience, he said that he felt he had perhaps caught some strange disease, albeit a pleasurable one, from which he hoped he would never recover. Venkataraman's experience was over. He got up as though nothing had happened, but his mind had changed forever. He could no longer busy himself with going to school, playing games or chatting with friends. His disinterest in all this was apparent. He had experienced the divine, and that filled every pore of his being.

Life, however, had to be gone through. His brother chided him for being indifferent towards his studies and insisted on his going to school. One day he was doing an imposition from Bain's English grammar when, 'the futility of it struck him with great force'. Putting aside his books he wrote a note to his mother which read, 'I have, in search of my Father and in obedience to His command, started from here. This is only embarking on a virtuous enterprise. Therefore, none need grieve over this affair.'

Ramana left for Tiruvannamalai. The town of Tiruvannamalai surrounds the mountain of Arunachala and is a major pilgrimage centre. Tiruvannamalai has one of the principal Siva lingam temples in South India.[1] Ramana, because he did not know the route, took three days to reach there and meditated in the basement of the Siva temple for six weeks. He had festered wounds, anthills growing on him and an emaciated body when they pulled him out of the temple. This was a dark, damp and dusty place where the patala linga was kept. Ramana was brought out by some people, looked after, and it would be no exaggeration to say he was actually brought back to life. Thereafter he spent all his life in and around the Arunachala mountain, staying for some time in the Virupaksha caves in the vicinity.

Yama kept visiting him off and on. Ramana learned to cope with Yama's visits more easily. They would last for even shorter periods. Once Ramana was on his way from the Virupaksha caves to Pachaiamman temple in Tiruvannamalai, accompanied by his disciples Palaniswami, Vasudeva Sastri and others. He had an oil bath there, and after some time returned. On their return, near a place called Tortoise Rock, Yama met Ramana.[2] Ramana has described the encounter:

> The landscape in front of me disappeared as a bright white curtain was drawn across my vision and shut it out. I could distinctly see the gradual process. There was a stage when I could still see a part of the landscape clearly while the rest was covered by the advancing curtain. On experiencing this I stopped walking lest I should fall. When it cleared I walked on. When darkness and faintness came over me a second time I leaned against a rock until it cleared. The third time it happened I felt it safer to sit, so I sat down near the rock. Then the bright white curtain completely shut off my vision, my head was swimming and my circulation and breathing stopped. The skin turned a livid blue. It was the regular death hue and it got darker and darker. Vasudeva Sastri, in fact, took me to be dead and held me in his arms and began to weep aloud and lament my death.

> I could distinctly feel his clasp and his shivering and hear his words of lamentation and understand their meaning. I also saw the discoloration of my skin and felt the stoppage of my circulation and breathing and the increased chilliness of the extremities of my body. My usual current of awareness still continued in that state also.
>
> I was not in the least afraid and felt no sadness at the condition of the body. I had sat down near the rock in my usual posture and closed my eyes and was not leaning against the rock. The body, left without circulation or respiration, still maintained that position. This state continued for some ten or fifteen minutes. Then a shock passed suddenly through the body and circulation revived with enormous force, and breathing also, and the body perspired from every pore. The colour of life reappeared on the skin. I then opened my eyes and got up and said, 'Let's go.' We reached Virupaksha Cave without further trouble. This was the only fit I had in which both circulation and respiration stopped.

Ramana was now thirty-two years old. The first time Yama met Ramana, he had been only sixteen. After that Yama did not meet Ramana, for it was not necessary. Ramana was one with the Eternal. Every time Ramana Maharishi spoke, it was the voice of the Eternal One. Ramana Maharishi encouraged his disciples to ask the question, 'Who am I?' Vaivaswata Yama had shown Ramana Maharishi the source.

And Ramana Maharishi urged all those who were interested in and ready to do the same to get to the source. He gave them, his followers, the method of self-enquiry, which was a very specific method for the individual to find out where the individual sense of 'I' arises. Self-enquiry is a method of active investigation, not one of passive witnessing. The answer is not conceptual. The only correct answer is in the form of a direct experience.[3]

Once a follower of Ramana Maharishi asked him, 'Why should self-enquiry alone be considered the direct path to realisation?'

Ramana Maharishi, addressed as Bhagwan by his followers, replied, 'Because every kind of path except self-enquiry presupposes the retention of the mind as the instrument for following it and cannot be followed without the mind. The ego may take different and more subtle forms at different stages of one's practice but it is never destroyed. The attempt to destroy the ego or the mind by methods other than self-enquiry is alike a thief turning a policeman to catch the thief himself ... He will go with you and pretend to catch the thief, but nothing will be gained. So, you must turn inward and see where the mind rises from and then it will cease to exist.'[4]

The enormous task of harnessing the mind was described in different ways by Ramana Maharishi.

Yama heard Ramana tell his followers a story. Yama recollected it in his own words:

If you have a bull for a pet and you leave the doors to its stable open, the bull will wander out. Not everyone will be kind to it, particularly if it begins to graze in someone else's fields or even home. It will be chased back. The next day, however, it will return to the fields, for it is bull-headed ... all it knows is to search for food in this manner, it does not recognise any boundaries. Ramana likened the bull to the mind ... just like the bull, the mind resents being tied down ... give it a mantra to do, japa, or sit it down to meditate, but soon after, the mind is wandering again. Self-enquiry, said Ramana, is like giving the bull a bundle of freshly cut grass. Give it plenty and fill its stable with it too. Then, even if the doors of the stable are left open it will not go out. If it still does, it will realise sooner or later that to face the torture of those who chase it back is not worth it because it has a ready supply of fresh, green grass right in the stable. Similarly, when the mind wanders, take it back to the stable, which is where the fodder is. Every time it goes out seeking pleasures in the world, it will get hurt. Bring it back to the source. This is self-enquiry. Eventually the mind will learn to stay inside and serious self-enquiry will begin.

Yama was happy to see many people working on Ramana's method. He reflected that Adi Shankaracharya had taught Advaita Vedanta too, emphasising the oneness of the Self and Brahman. Shankara focused on jnana yoga (path of knowledge), using scriptural analysis and logical reasoning to establish Brahman as the sole reality.[5] Ramana had simplified it into a direct self-inquiry (Who am I?), advocating experiential realisation over intellectual study.

Once the source is found, thought Yama, then what Narayana, in his incarnation as Krishna had told Arjuna, will make sense at so many levels:

> The wise grieve neither for the living nor the dead
> Just as the soul passes from childhood to youth to old age,
> So too does it pass into another body after death[6]

With a sense of accomplishment, Yama mounted Mahisha on his journey back to Yamaloka, humming:

> Bhaja Govindam, bhaja Govindam, Govindam bhaja moodamathe
> Samprapte sannihite kale nahi nahi rakshati dukrinjnkarane[7]

(Immerse yourself in Govinda, worship Govinda, you fool, these rules of grammar will come to your rescue when you face Death)

Book 8

THE IMMORTAL

37
Yama meets mortality

Yama was sauntering about on Mahisha, feeling the pleasant onset of spring. The earth was also happy, like him. Flowers were blooming, birds were chirping and the sky was clear. Suddenly he saw a little girl, maybe about six or seven years old, sitting on the low parapet wall of the veranda of her house. Her legs were dangling and her face was covered by her unruly crop of hair.

Just as Yama saw her, she too caught sight of him.

'Are you Yama?' she asked.

Bidding Mahisha to stop, Yama got down and went close to her. 'Yes, I am,' he said, bending down to her face with a smile, speaking gently.

The little child looked up into his eyes and her own filled with tears. 'Why did you take my father?' she asked.

A younger child was visible through the door that was ajar. So was a distraught mother.

Yama's heart stopped. None of what he had told Nachiketas, Savitri, Yudhishthira, Ramana ... could this moment hold. It was too full of grief.

With his hand Yama gestured to the child to move a little and give him space. He sat next to her on the parapet and took her hand in his. They both cried together.

Maybe tomorrow he can tell her something more, thought Yama. That her father's love is immortal. The beauty of his love is immortal. And that they, his love and the beauty in their relationship, would always be with her. He would show her the beautiful gulmohar tree in full bloom and show the same to her when the flowers had fallen. And then he would tell her, 'The object of beauty does not remain. It may be destroyed or perish. But beauty remains. In our eyes, in our mind, in our experiences. The world has existed for a long time. Objects of beauty have come and gone. No object has remained forever. But it is the magic of its beauty that has spread itself in the memory of the earth to make the earth a beautiful place to live in. It is also the inspiration for beauty to keep getting created and recreated.

'Just like that, your father's love is what makes him precious to you. His love is always with you, it can never die. You will, in turn, spread that love to others – to your sibling, your friends, your family, your co-workers, your pets ... everyone. Once a person is born, he or she never dies. He just changes form and in the process of doing so leaves infinite love behind. This love is immortal. Just as beauty is immortal. Procreation is a gross aspect of the continuity of mankind. In love and beauty, the essence, the spirit of the world, keeps the continuity.

'Look into your heart and you will find your father. Show everyone your father through your love, your beauty – the beauty in your being, not material beauty. All that is material will have to go away one day or another.

'Life is like a relay race, where love and beauty make the baton. They, love and beauty, are radiant and eternal. Some call this a glimpse of Brahman. Some call it your father. Shine forth. That is the essence of life and of immortality.'

Yama took a deep breath. For today, he just let her lean on him and drop off to sleep.

Epilogue

The one who supports and sustains the earth
The one who provides food for all life on it
The one who fills the skies with the water of life
The one who holds the suns and heavens above

By that same Brahman alone
I too will tide over Death and become eternal

The one who turns the wheels of time and makes a
year
The one who within that year, twelve months creates
The one whose order of day and night
Is not transgressed by them

By that same Brahman alone
I too will tide over Death and become eternal

The one who is the life source of all life givers
The one whose regions of the universe are full of
prosperity
The one whose light radiates and holds

Life in all quarters of space

By that same Brahman alone
I too will tide over Death and become eternal

The one from whose perfect nature and creativity
The nectar of immortality flows out
The one who is the lord and master of the sun-filled
joy of existence
The one in whose omniscience all the Vedas are
treasured

By that same Brahman alone
I too will tide over Death and become eternal.

'Atimrtyu Sukta', *Atharva Veda* 4.35

Notes

INTRODUCTION

1 Sudhamahi Regunathan, *Siku: Faith and Conversion – Donyipolo Movement in Arunachal Pradesh* (Har Anand Publications, 2000).

2 The four stages or ashramas in a human being's life, according to traditional Hindu thought, are brahmacharya (studenthood), grihastha (life as a householder), vanaprastha (life of retreat in the forest) and sanyasa (renunciation).

3 *Prajnanam Brahma* (Consciousness is Brahman) from the *Aitareya Veda*, *Aham Brahmasmi* (I am Brahman) from the *Brihadaranyaka Upanishad*, *Tat Tvam Asi* (You are That) from the *Chandogya Upanishad* and *Ayam Atma Brahma* (This Self is Brahman) from the *Mandukya Upanishad* are considered to be the mahavakyas, or the great truths.

4 A heroine mentioned in the Mahabharata, 'Vana Parva', celebrated for her beauty and love for Nala (her husband). Their love is put to many tests and proven to be steadfast.

CHAPTER 1 THE MAKING OF YAMA

1 *Rig Veda*, Mandala 10, hymn 10.

2 In some places her name is given as Saranyu, as in the *Rig Veda*, and in some as Sanjna (pronounced 'Sangya'), as in all versions of the *Markandeya Purana*.

3 *The Markandeya Purana*, translated by F. Eden Pargiter, edited by K.L. Joshi (Parimal Publications, 1904, 2004), Chapter 74, verses 3 and 4, p. 351. The original verse in Sanskrit reads:

> मयि दृष्टे सदा यस्मात्कुरुषे नेत्रसंयमम् ।
> तस्माउ्जनिष्यसे मूढे प्रजासंयमनं यमम् ॥ ४॥

Praja samyamanam yamam has been translated as Yama the imprisoner of mankind and the destroyer of mankind in another translation by Partiger alone (published by Baptist Mission Press, 1904). I would think it means 'Yama, the restrainer of living beings'.

4 The word Yama also means twin. In Indo-European mythology, Yama's twin was Manu. The story told therein is that Manu sacrificed Yama so that mortal life on earth may begin.

5 There is some ambiguity about who Soorya was. Scholars have different views. Sukumari Bhattacharji, in her book *The Indian Theogony*, says she is Savitr's daughter and that Savitr is more an idea than a phenomenon. 'Soorya is Savitr's daughter ... Like Surya, Savitr is golden armed, golden eyed, everything about Savitr is beautiful ... none of the other sun-gods, not even his enemies, can measure Savitr's dominion ... (p. 214). Later in the book, Soorya is mentioned as possibly a feminine and softer form of the Sun himself. 'Thus Surya and Soorya would appear as mutually convertible forms of the sun, the conversion only emphasized certain traits; power and brilliance in the masculine form, warmth, charm and mildness in the feminine form' (p. 225).

6 *Rig Veda*, Mandala 10, hymn 85.37. Known as the 'Bridal Hymn', this hymn continues to be used in marriage rituals in some communities of India. Some features described in the hymn are still in practice in Hindu marriage rituals.

7 Surya is believed to have had two sons, Vaivaswata Manu and Yama, and a daughter, Yami, with Sanjna. Later Sanjna bore him the twins the Ashvins. With Chhaya he had Savarni Manu, Shani (Saturn) and a daughter, Tapti. There is also mention in mythology of more sons of Surya, such as Karna and Sugriva.

CHAPTER 2 YAMA AND YAMI

1 Sometimes mentioned as brothers and sometimes as close associates.

2 *Rig Veda*, Mandala 10, hymn 3:37.
3 Ibid., Mandala 3, hymn 59:1 and Mandala 8, hymn 25:9.
4 *Rig Veda*, Mandala 1, hymn 179.
5 Traditionally, it is believed that a man should have a son to perform his last rites.
6 The story is told up to this point in the *Rig Veda*, Mandala 10, hymn 10. The story of how Yama died is not given in the *Rig Veda*. It just states that he was the first to die. The story of what happens to Yami when he dies is told in the *Maitryani Samhita* of the *Yajur Veda*, Kanda 1, Prapathaka 5, anuvaka 12.
7 S.N. Khandelwal, *Brihaddharma Puranam* (Chowkhamba Sanskrit Series Office, 2014), Chapter 60, verses 1–14, p. 352. The story goes on to say that Parvati was disheartened. So Siva took Parvati's clothes and made a doll for her. The rag doll had the face of an elephant. Parvati took the doll to her breast and, lo and behold, it came to life and Ganesha was born.
8 *Rig Veda*, Mandala 10, hymn 96.
9 *Maitryani Samhita* of the *Yajur Veda*, Kanda 1, Prapathaka 5, anuvaka 12.
10 Chinnaswami Shastri and Pattabhirama Shastri, *Tandya Maha Brahmana* (Chowkhamba Sanskrit Sansthan, 1987), Chapter 11, verse 10:21–22.

CHAPTER 3 YAMA, THE KING

1 One yojana is 8–9 kilometres.
2 *Rig Veda*, Mandala 10, hymn 14.
3 Matulanga (*Citrus medica*) is a citrus fruit, known variously in India as baranimbu, bijaura, kadaranarattai, naarthankai, thurinjippazham, madiaphalamu and turanj. It is high in vitamin C and is used in many medicinal preparations.

CHAPTER 4 A DAY IN YAMAPURI

1 *Brahmanda Purana*, translated and annotated by G.V. Tagare (Motilal Banarasidas Publishers, 2002), p. 201, 1.2.21.31–38.
2 Angiras was a teacher of divine knowledge, a mediator between men and gods. In other hymns he is the first

of the Agni-devas. The Angirases are his descendants. They are mentioned by some scholars as Yama's messengers. Navagvas are also Angirases. Atharvan, also a contemporary of Angiras, is considered the author of the *Atharva Veda*. His followers were called Atharvans. Similarly Bhrigus were the descendants of Bhrigu, the mind-born son of Brahma.

3 *Rig Veda*, Mandala 10, hymn 14.
4 Ibid., hymn 10.
5 Ibid., Mandala 1, hymn 164.46.
6 Dikpalas are guardians of the directions. Kubera, the God of Wealth, guards the north, Yama the south. Indra, the King of Heavens, the east, and Varuna the west. Northeast is Ishana, southeast is Agni, Vayu is to the northwest and Nritta to the southwest.
7 *Atharva Veda*, Kanda 6, sukta 84.1.

CHAPTER 5 YAMA AND AGNI

1 In the Vedas Varuna represented all this. But in the Upanishadic times Varuna got linked more to water.
2 This story is told in the *Shatapatha Brahmana* 1.3.3.13.
3 *Rig Veda: Mandala 10*, commentary by Pandit Harishchandra Vidyalankar and Acharya Vaidyanath Shastri ji (Sarvadeshik Arya Pratinidhi Sabha, 2010), hymn 51, pp. 674–676.
4 *Mahabharata Adi Parva*, translated by Manmatha Nath Dutt (New Delhi: H.C. Das Elysium Press), Chapter 199, p. 268.
5 *Rig Veda*, Mandala 10, hymn 10.
6 *Atharva Veda*, translated by Tulsi Ram (Vijaykumar Govindram Hasanand, 2013), Kanda 18, sukta 2, verse 32. p. 542.

CHAPTER 6 YAMA AND MARKANDEYA

1 Story associated with Azhagar Kovil near Tiruchirappalli. Grateful for the little intervention that Vishnu did for him, Yama is believed to propitiate Vishnu in this temple every day, to this day. He had requested Vishnu and

Lakshmi to reside in this temple. This place is also known as Kallazhagar temple, and the Vishnu here is known as Sunderaja Perumal, or the beautiful-looking god.

2 The Vaitarani is believed to be a river of blood and filth that separates earth from the kingdom of Yama. Crossing the Vaitarani is a metaphor used to communicate how difficult it is to reach a safe abode after death. If one has lived righteously, the waters are welcoming; if one has made enough sacrifices, particularly of a cow, one is ferried across, and so on. These beliefs associated with the river may be purely metaphoric.

3 I worship that effervescent Shiva of three eyes, the one who nourishes us. As from its stem the cucumber is separated, falls off, so too may I be released from death and connected to my source (*Rig Veda*, 7.59.12).

4 The story is told in many places and has been assembled here mainly from *Padma Purana*, Mahabharata and *Linga Purana*.

5 The Vedic worldview was focused on rituals and natural forces. Death was seen as a transition, and Yama's role was largely neutral, or even positive.

6 In the *Rig Veda*, there is no clear mention of hell. In *Agni Purana*, four hells are mentioned in some recensions and seven in some others; in *Manu Smriti* and *Yajnavalkya Smriti* twenty-one hells are mentioned; and in the *Bhagvata Purana* and *Garuda Purana*, there are twenty-eight names for different types of hells, with many other hell-like places described.

7 The story of Vijaya is told in Chapter 3.

CHAPTER 7 YAMA AS ANTAKA

1 The story of Dadanc is mentioned in the *Rig Veda* and references are found in the Mahabharata and the Puranas too. The story told here is collated from all of them. Sometimes Dadanc is thought to be the same as Rishi Dadichi. Dadichi was a sage who had observed such

severe austerities that his bones were very strong. When Indra had to slay the demon Vritra, he was told only Dadichi's bones were strong enough to make his vajra, or thunderbolt. So Dadichi is said to have sacrificed his life for the good of the world.

2 Swami Vivekananda, *Reflections* (Om Books International, 2017) pp. 193–194.

3 Vishnu Sharman, *Panchatantra* (Motilal Banarasidass Publishers, 2012). Story from the last section of *Aparikshatakarakani*.

4 Scholars say the *Garuda Purana* was begun sometime in the first century CE and worked upon every now and then till the eleventh or twelfth century.

5 When the later mythological sections of the epics and Puranas were being composed, there was great emphasis on the doctrine of reincarnation, the concept of an impersonal Brahman, the personal soterial god Isvara, the authority of the Smritis (religious conventions) and Srutis (the Vedas) and emergence of the triad of Brahma, Vishnu and Siva.

6 J.L. Shastri, *Linga Purana* (Motilal Publishers Pvt. Ltd, 1993), 1.30.

7 Mahabharata, 'Vana Parva', 'Tirtha-yatra Parva', 142.36–44. The verse numbers given for the Mahabharata follow the Sanskrit text of the Mahabharata translated by Manmatha Nath Dutt (Parimal Trust, 2001) though many other versions have also been consulted.

8 'Maha Mrityunjaya Mantra', *Rig Veda*, 7.59.12.

CHAPTER 8 DHUMORNA WAITS FOR YAMA

1 Priyabala Shah, *Sri Vishnudharmottara* (New Order Book Co., 1990), 3.35.1–5.

2 *The Garuda Purana*, translated by Ernest Wood and S.V Subrahmanyam (Panini Office, Bhuvaneswari Ashrama, 1911), Chapter 14, verses 31–33.

3 Ibid., verse 74–75.

4 Ibid., Chapter 3, verses 19–21.

5 The word used to describe Nachiketas in the second verse of the *Kathopanishad* is Kumara. Kumara refers to a boy who is above the age of five and below the age of twelve. Different commentators have chosen different ages for Nachiketas. Considering the seriousness of his conversations with his father and with Yama, and considering his knowledge of how rituals are to be performed, most commentators tend to locate his age between nine and twelve years.

6 *Kathopanishad*, 1.1.7 and 1.1.8. In none of the versions of the original does it say who said this to Yama. Maybe his guard, Dhumorna, or someone else.

CHAPTER 9 YAMA MEETS NACHIKETAS

1 Vedanta Society of New York, '2. Katha Upanishad | Mantras 1.1.1 - 3 | Swami Sarvapriyananda', YouTube. Available online: https://www.youtube.com/watch?v=MmoxzLIzAas (accessed 23 July 2025).

2 *Rig Veda*, Mandala 10, hymn 117.

3 Swami Chinmayananda, *Discourses on Kathopanishad* (Chinmaya Publication Trust, 1963), p. 7.

4 There is an opinion among some scholars that Nachiketas asked the question because he saw his father was giving away everything he possessed and he felt it would be natural that he would be given away too. There are two reasons why the other argument appears more plausible: 1) Why the special mention in the account that the cows that were being given away were weak and unhealthy? That would be mentioned only if there were better, healthier ones that could be given away. 2) It is difficult to believe that Nachiketas, who three days later would ask such profound questions of Yama, would be so naive.

5 *Kathopanishad*, Chapter 1, mantra 6, in *Eight Upanishads with the Commentary of Shankaracharya*, translated by Swami Gambhirananda, Volume 1 (Advaita Ashrama, 2002). All verse numbers are from this book, while many others have been consulted too.

6 Ibid., mantra 5.
7 Ibid., mantra 9.
8 Ibid., mantra 10.
9 *Brahma Purana*, Parts 1–4 (Motilal Banarasidass, 1955), Chapter 2, verses 29–30.
10 Yama refers to him as Audalakki, son of Aruna. Swami Gambhirananda says Audalakki is the same as Uddalak, another name for Vajasravasva. Vajasravasa is also reffered to as Gautama in some verses in the *Kathopanishad*.
11 *Kathopanishad*, Chapter 1.11.

CHAPTER 10 YAMA GRANTS NACHIKETAS HIS SECOND BOON

1 *Kathopanishad*, Chapter 1, verses 12–13.
2 Sri Aurobindo, 'Agni: The Divine Will Force,' *CWSA*, Vol. 15, pp. 388–389.
3 Swami Sarvapriyananda, *Katha Upanishad*, Lecture 5, https://www.youtube.com/watch?v=1Of2oh_V1uc.
4 *Kathopanishad*, Chapter 1.1.14.
5 The term used is Srikam Anekarupam. Some scholars say it means a variegated gold necklace, while others wonder what use a little boy asking such spiritual questions would have for a gold necklace. They say it means the path.
6 *Kathopanishad*, Chapter 1.1.16.
7 While the *Kathopanishad* just says that Yama taught Nachiketas what the fire altar will look like and how many bricks it should be made of, etc., it does not describe Yama saying how it is made. However, the qualifications of the one who is perfoming the yajna, the procedure and the result are elaborated in two mantras, *Kathopanishad*, 1.1.17 and 1.1.18.
8 *Kathopanishad*, 1.1.19.

CHAPTER 11 NACHIKETAS ASKS FOR HIS THIRD BOON

1 *Kathopanishad*, 1.1.20.
2 Ibid., 1.1.21.
3 Ibid., 1.1.22.

4 Ibid., 1.1.23.
5 Ibid., 1.1.24.
6 *Mahabharata* (BORI Edition), 'Adi Parva', Chapters 15–30.
7 *Eight Upanishads with the Commentary of Shankaracharya*, translated by Swami Gambhirananda, Volume 1, 1.1.25. The translation by Swami Gambhirananda goes thus:
What things that are desirable but difficult to get – pray for all those cherished things according to your choice
here are these women with chariots and musical instruments – such are surely not to be had by mortals
with these, who are offered by me, you get yourself served
O Nachiketa, do not enquire about death.
This has been reproduced here so the reader may know of the small liberties I have taken with my translation.
8 *The Garuda Purana*, chapter 16.29.
9 Ibid., 33
10 Ibid., 53.
11 *Eight Upanishads*, 1.1.26–29.
12 This is the Shanti mantra preceding the *Kathopanishad*. It also occurs at the end of Chapter 1, valli 3. *Maa vidvissaavahai* is translated as 'may we not cavil at each other' by Swami Gambhirananda and as 'may we not hate each other' by Swami Chinmayananda. And shanti, meaning peace, has been retained in this translation.

CHAPTER 12 YAMA TESTS THE STUDENT

1 It is not clearly mentioned in the Mahabharata as to who Dharma was. In the *Puranic Encyclopedia*, edited by Vettam Mani (Motilal Banarasidass, 1979), it is said that Dharma and Kala are different entities (p. 224). Kala is the same as Yama (ibid., p. 369). It is also mentioned in the entry on Dharma that the name is used interchangeably with Yama throughout the Mahabharata, but Dharma is the offspring of Brahma, while Yama is the son of Surya and Sanjna. When Yama is used to denote Dharma, it is because Yama means self-control. However,

the difference is difficult to make out in the stories. And Yama is called Dharmaraja.

2 Swami Gambhirananda in his translation refers to Shreyas as the preferable or electable and Preyas as the pleasurable or delectable. Swami Chinmayananda calls them good and pleasant. Patrick Olivelle calls them good and gratifying.

3 *Eight Upanishads*, 1.2.1–2.

4 Ibid., 1.2.3.

5 Ibid., 1.2.4–6.

6 Mahabharata, 'Anushasana Parva', 1.1–1.5.

7 *Eight Upanishads*, 1.2.7.

CHAPTER 13 YAMA REVEALS THE TRUTH

1 See Note 1, Chapter 5.

2 Mahabharata, 'Ashvamedha Parva', Chapter 13.

3 The reference here is to adhyatma yoga. Swami Savrapriyananda defines adhyatma yoga as gyana yoga, as centring oneself in pure consciousness, in the clarity that 'I am Brahman'.

4 Mahabharata, 'Aswamedha Parva', chapter 13:2.

5 *Eight Upanishads*, 1.2.8–9.

6 Ibid., 1.2.10.

7 The destination is the limit that one can attain. According to the Vedas, in a series of heavens, this is the ultimate, the final, the last. Swami Gambhirananda (*Eight Upanishads*, p. 144) refers to this as the Hiranyagarbha. His translation is presented here: 'O Nachiketa, you on becoming enlightened have rejected them all by examining patiently the highest reach of desire, the support of the universe, the infinite results of meditation, the other shore of fearlessness, the extensive course [of Hiranyagarbha] that is praiseworthy and great, as also [your own] state.' Swami Sarvapriyananda says that for each cycle of the Universe there is only one Hiranyagarbha Brahma depending on which individual has accumulated the maximum good karmas.

8 *Eight Upanishads*, 1.2.11.
9 Ibid., chapter 1.2.12–13.

CHAPTER 14 THIS INDEED IS THAT, SAID YAMA

1 The life of a student or seeker.
2 According to Patrick Olivelle (*Upanishads*: *A New Translation*, Oxford University Press, 2008. p. 237), here ends the dialogue between Yama and Nachiketas..
3 This mahavakya, or great truth, occurs in the first part of the second chapter of the *Kathopanishad*.
4 Mahabharata, 'Ashvamedhika Parva', I.
5 *Eight Upanishads*, 1.3.3, 4, 5 and 9.
6 Ibid., 1.3.10–12.
7 Ibid., 1.3.13.
8 Ibid., 1.3.14–15.
9 There is a strong argument that the conversation between Yama and Nachiketas ends here and that the second chapter of *Kathopanishad* was added to fill in the gaps or questions that arose from this discussion. Swami Chinmayananda, *Kathopanishad*, Section 3, pp. 152–153.

CHAPTER 15 YAMA LEAVES YAMAPURI

1 *Mahabharata* (BORI edition), 'Vana Parva', Chapter 278, verses 3–5.
2 Ibid., verse 15.
3 Ibid., verse 22.
4 Ibid., Chapter 279, verse 8.
5 Ibid., Chapter 280, verse 9.
6 Ibid., verse 10.
7 Ibid., verse 17.
8 The triratra vow is described in Chapter 70 of the *Padma Purana*. Rishi Narada asks Mahesha what one can do so that one does not suffer grief. That is when Siva, or Mahesha, describes the nadi-triratra vow, which entails fasting for three days and nights. By observing this vow, the practitioner does not go to hell. A man obtains a long

life, good health, good fortune, happiness, wealth and progeny, and is honoured in heaven.

9 *Mahabharata* (BORI edition), 'Vana Parva', Chapter 280, verse 32.

CHAPTER 16 YAMA ARRIVES IN SHALVA FOREST

1 Mahabharata (BORI edition), 'Vana Parva', Chapter 281, verses 3–5.

2 Ibid., verse 6.

3 Soon after she had attained puberty she was considered marriageable and sent to look for a groom.

4 *Mahabharata* (BORI edition), 'Vana Parva', Chapter 281, verse 8.

5 Ibid., verse 9.

6 To bring the palms together in a namaste.

7 *Mahabharata* (BORI edition), 'Vana Parva', Chapter 281, verse 10.

8 The story of Savitri and Satyavan is told by Rishi Markandeya to Yudhishthira in the 'Vana Parva' of the Mahabharata. Yudhishthira, overcome by sorrow that his wife Draupadi has to suffer with them when they were in exile, asks Markandeya, 'Have you heard of any woman as good and noble as Draupadi who faced such tribulations?' In answer to that, Markandeya relates this story of how a lady devoted to her husband ennobled herself despite the odds of fate.

9 *Mahabharata* (BORI edition), 'Vana Parva', Chapter 281, verse 11.

10 Ibid., verse 12.

11 Widows were considered inauspicious, and a young widow more so.

12 *Mahabharata* (BORI edition), 'Vana Parva', Chapter 281, verse 13.

13 Ibid., verse 14.

14 Ibid., verse 15.

15 Ibid., verse 16.

16 Ibid., verse 18.
17 Ibid., verse 19.

CHAPTER 17 YAMA JOURNEYS BACK

1 Shri Aurobindo describes the thumb-sized being which Yama yanks out of Satyavan as a luminous Satyavan rising from the mortal coil.
2 Rohit Mehta, *The Dialogue with Death* (Sri Aurobindo Ashram Book Distribution Agency, 1972), p. 272.
3 *The Garuda Purana*, 1.56–57.
4 *Mahabharata* (BORI edition), 'Vana Parva', Chapter 281, verse 20.
5 Ibid., verse 21.
6 Ibid., verse 22.
7 Saptapadi, the seven steps taken by the groom and bride, solemnise a marriage. With each step, a vow is taken for matrimonial harmony and acceptance of duties.
8 *Mahabharata* (BORI edition), 'Vana Parva', Chapter 281, verses 23–24.
9 *Sri Vishnu Purana* (Gita Press, 1990), Book 3, Chapter 7, 'Yama Gita', verse 16.
10 Ibid., verse 20. In this chapter, the story is told of how Nakula, one of the Pandava princes, asked Bhishma, his grandfather, if there was any way of evading the clutches of Yama. Bhishma tells him that he once met a realised brahmin from Kalinga to whom he had put this very same question. That brahmin had told him of a secret conversation he had overheard between Yama and his messenger. Yama had whispered these words into the ears of the messenger. While the instructions given by Yama are long, the core message is as given in the verse above.
11 *Mahabharata* (BORI edition), 'Vana Parva', Chapter 281, verse 25.
12 Ibid., verse 26.
13 Ibid., verse 27.

CHAPTER 18 YAMA AND NARAYANA

1 *Mahabharata* (BORI edition), 'Vana Parva', Chapter 281, verse 28.
2 Ibid., verse 29.
3 G.V. Tagare, *Bhagvata Purana* (Motilal Banarasidass, 1999), Canto 6, Chapter 1.
4 *The Garuda Purana (Saroddhara)*, translated by Ernest Wood and S.V. Subrahmanyam (Panini Office Bhuvaneswari Ashrama, 1911), 1.11.
5 Ibid., 1.6.
6 *Mahabharata* (BORI edition), 'Vana Parva', Chapter 281, verse 30.
7 Ibid., verse 31.
8 Ibid., verse 32.

CHAPTER 19 HOW YAMA FUNCTIONS

1 The word Yama means rein in or curb or keep under control. It is the first of the eight limbs of yoga. It also means moral discipline.
2 *Mahabharata* (BORI edition), 'Vana Parva', Chapter 281, verse 33.
3 Ibid., verses 34–35.
4 *The Garuda Purana*, 3.8–13.
5 Ibid., 3.16.
6 Ibid., 3.17.
7 *Mahabharata* (BORI edition), 'Vana Parva', Chapter 281, verse 36.
8 Ibid., verse 37.
9 Ibid., verse 38.
10 Ibid., verses 40–42.
11 Ibid., verse 43.
12 Ibid., verse 44.
13 Ibid., verse 45.
14 Ibid., verse 46.
15 Ibid., verse 47.

16 कालो ऽस्मि लोकक्षयकृत् प्रवृद्धो लोकान् समाहर्तुम् इह प्रवृत्तः । Bhagavad Gita, 11.32.
17 *Mahabharata* (BORI edition), 'Vana Parva', Chapter 281, verses 48–49.
18 Ibid., verse 50.

CHAPTER 20 YAMA DECIDES

1 *Mahabharata* (BORI edition), 'Vana Parva', Chapter 281, verses 55–58.
2 Ibid., verse 63.
3 Ibid., verse 64.
4 Ibid., Chapter 282, verses 37–39.
5 When Rishi Markandeya had finished relating this story to Yudhishthira, Rishi Vaishampayana added, 'The one who listens to this story of Savitri with reverence will find happiness and success in every endeavour and will never have to embrace misery.' Rishi Vaishampayana was the poet to whom Vyasa had taught the Mahabharata after he composed it. *Mahabharata* (BORI edition), 'Vana Parva', Chapter 283, verse 17.

CHAPTER 21 THE LIFE-GIVER

1 *Mahabharata* (BORI Edition), 'Sambhava Parva', Chapter 123, verse 4.
2 A sage had cursed King Pandu that if he ever embraced a woman he would meet his death. Therefore his wives Kunti and Madri could not bear children.
3 After Kunti gave birth to Yudhishthira, she had two more sons, Bhima by Indra, King of the Heavens, and Arjuna by Vayu, or wind. She taught the mantra to Madri, who bore two sons, Nakula and Sahdeva, offspring of the Ashvins.

CHAPTER 22 THE YAKSHA

1 The questions put to Yudhishthira by the yaksha and his responses follow the Sanskrit text of the Mahabharata translated by Manmatha Nath Dutt (Parimal Trust, 2001). They begin from Chapter 311 of the 'Arenya Parva' in the 'Vana Parva' and go on up to Chapter 315. The main

reference is this one, though many other versions and editions have been consulted too.

2 Mahabharata, 'Vana Parva', 'Arenya Parva', Chapter 313, verses 20–22.

3 The original verse asks, 'By what does one have a second?' Dutt (*Mahabharata*) translates it without explaining second *of what*. Bibek Debroy (*Sacred Songs: The Mahabharata's Many Gitas*, Rupa Publications, 2023) says second could mean second in the family, a son. And then the answer 'perseverance', as given by Yudhishthira, will fit. There is also a view that the second implies a partner, companion. However, I think that by second is meant a second chance, as Sunita or Vena got. Then perseverance will be the right answer.

4 The Vedas, the Brahmanas, the Aranyakas and the Upanishads are called the Shruti texts. Through learning the Shruti texts, one becomes learned.

5 The word used is dhriti, which means holding, supporting, keeping, maintaining (Monier Williams, *A Sanskrit-English Dictionary*, Motilal Banarasidass, 1963).

6 Mahabharata, 'Shanti Parva', Chapter 192.

CHAPTER 23 YAMA AND ARJUNA

1 Swadhyaya is more than just study. It is virtuous observance, study of the self, study of the Vedas, and can be said to have three stages: shravana (hearing); manana (learning by heart); nidhidhyasana (internalising and reflecting).

2 The story appears in the Mahabharata, 'Karna Parva', Chapter 69. It is told by Krishna to Arjuna to illustrate that some people, even though they wish to gain religious merit, lose it all by using their erudition and will in the wrong manner.

3 Guhyakas are literally the hidden ones who live in caves and are generally associated with Kubera. Gandharvas are celestial performers. Nagas are associated with the snake, sometimes half-snake, half-human, sometimes representing the underworld as snakes live underground. So the three worlds are covered.

4 Mahanubahu literally means the great one with long arms. But it is generally a term of adoration used to describe a great being.

5 Mahabharata, 'Adi Parva', 'Kirata Parva', Chapter 41, verses 4–24.

CHAPTER 24 YAMA AS A CALF

1 Some of the next few questions were:
Yama: What is the single sacrificial recitation?
Yudhishthira: The breath is the single sacrificial recitation.
Yama: What is the single sacrificial principle?
Yudhishthira: The mind is the single sacrificial principle.
Yama: What is the single thing sacrifices need?
Yudhishthira: Speech is the single thing that sacrifices need.
Yama: And what is it that sacrifice cannot transgress?
Yudhishthira: Sacrifices cannot transgress speech.

2 In a beautiful explanation in *The Secret of the Vedas* (Sri Aurobindo Ashram, 2018), Sri Aurobindo says that the word 'go' or 'gava', though meaning cow literally, is used to represent knowledge, light and wealth. When it refers to something physical, it means wealth. Symbolically, it is knowledge, which is light. Though most translations interpret Yudhishthira's answer gavaha to mean cow, I think knowledge fits better.

3 In Sanskrit the word used is Putr … it could mean son, it could mean child. I prefer to understand it as child.

4 Sri Aurobindo, *Secret of the Vedas*, Chapter 8, p. 88.

5 G.V. Tagare, *Bhagvata Purana* (Motilal Banarasidass, 1999), Chapter 18.

6 Mahabharata, 'Drona Parva', Chapter 69.

CHAPTER 25 YAMA, YAYATI AND YAMUNA

1 *Padmapurana*, translated and annotated by N.A. Deshpande (Motilal Banarasidass Publishers, 1990), Chapters 76–78.

2 A legend commonly believed and narrated in North India.

CHAPTER 26 YAMA AND NRGA

1 Based on the second story from the last section of the *Panchatantra* titled 'Aparikshitakarakani'.

2 The word used is bharya. Bharya has come to be synonymous with wife. The word is derived from the root bhr, which means to bear, carry, to support, sustain, to nourish, maintain. Bharya is one who has to be cherished, nurtured, carried along. It does not specifically mean wife, in my opinion. The term used for wife in the Vedic texts is patni.

3 This answer in the text is commonly translated as 'physician' but the Sanskrit word used is bhishak, which means healer. In the *Rig Veda* (10.97), the word is used to describe a divine healer.

4 Sthala Purana of Airavateswara temple, Darasuram.

5 The Ramayana, chapter 53 of the Uttarakanda, also tells a similar story. The version related here is primarily from the Mahabharata, 'Anushasana Parva', Chapter 118.

6 Ibid., 120–121.

7 The translation given by Manmatha Nath Dutt (*Mahabharata*, Volumes 1–9, Parimal Publications, 2001) reads:

> Agni is the guest of all creatures; the milk of the cows is Amrita
> Homa with Amrita is the eternal religion; and air is the entire Universe.

My translation is with reference to Sri Aurobindo's interpretation in *The Secret of the Vedas* (p. 355). *Somo gavamrtam*, the second part of the first line, is thus translated as the light of divine bliss is the amrita. According to Sri Aurobindo, soma as the intoxicating drink is the physical meaning. Symbolically, 'Soma, the Lord of the Ananda is the true creator who possesses the soul and brings out of it a divine creation. The mind and heart, enlightened, have formed into a purifying instrument; freed from all narrowness and duality the consciousness in it has been widely extended to receive the full flow of sense life and mind life and turn it into pure delight of true existence, the divine immortal Ananda. The soma wine of life comes pouring into all the members of the human system as into a wine jar … as the body becomes full of the touch and exultation of strong wine, so with this divine Ananda.' The next half line reads: *Sanatano amrito dharmo* … this should, by the same argument, be Ananda is the eternal religion.

'Vayu was considered to be a great force pervading all material existence and the condition of its activities … it is this idea that was formulated later on in the conception of Prana, the universal breath of Life. All the vital and nervous activities of the human being fall within the definition of Prana and belong to the domain of Vayu (*The Secret of the Vedas*, p. 309). To translate vayu as air would limit the idea.

CHAPTER 27 YAMA AND NALA

1 Mahabharata, 'Vana Parva', Chapters 55–57, pp. 158–164.
2 Atman, in my opinion, does not mean soul in this context. It means very dear, alter ego, that which is closest to one. Rain supported the life of man as in those times it was a primarily agrarian economy based on rain-fed cultivation of crops. The word used is danam, which literally means charity. I think generosity fits better here in translation.

CHAPTER 28 YAMA AND RAVANA

1 *Valmikyi Ramayanam* (Gita Press, 2019), 'Uttarakhanda', Chapter 20.
2 This question is asked after the four sets of questions earlier asked. The order, however, is different in different manuscripts. Some words also differ, and the number of questions is also not the same.

CHAPTER 29 YAMA AND HARISHCHANDRA

1 Shraddha means funerary rites. Yajna is collective prayer.
2 While this reference is found in the Mahabharata, the whole story of Harishchandra is told in the *Markandeya Purana*.

The *Markandeya Purana*, it is said, was written to explain some fundamental doubts that arose in Rishi Jaimini's mind after reading the Mahabharata. One of the characters about whom more is told is Harishchandra.

CHAPTER 30 YAMA AND SHIBI

1 The answer to the question 'What gives us food?' is given as cow in many translations. I tend to agree with some scholars who have interpreted it as Earth, for Earth did take the form of a cow to rejuvenate itself. Bibek Debroy (*Sacred Songs*, Rupa Publications, 2023) in his translation of *Yaksha Prashna* says the word Brahmana in the answer refers to *Brahma muhurta*, the early morning hours. In other translations it is interpreted as 'when a good brahmin is available'. Whether it means availability of a brahmin or the early hours of the morning, both seem right in their own way, as the good time to perform funerary rites.

2 Mahabharata, 'Sabha Parva', Chapter 8.

CHAPTER 31 YAMA AND RAMA

1 Vamana avatar, or the incarnation of Vishnu as a dwarf, was the fifth incarnation of Vishnu, which was taken to defeat King Bali.

2 *Valmiki Ramayanam*, Uttarakhanda, sarga 103–110. These sargas, however, come under the category of interpolated cantos.

CHAPTER 33 YAMA AND VIDURA

1 Mahabharata, 'Sambhava Parva', Chapter 108.

2 Mahabharata, 'Asramavasika Parva', Chapters 26 to 28.

3 *Valmiki Ramayanam*, Uttarakanda, Chapter 18.

CHAPTER 34 THE MOST FEARED KING

1 *The Garuda Purana (Saroddhara)*, translated by Ernest Wood and S.V. Subrahmanyam (Panini Office Bhuvaneswari Ashrama, 1911), Chapter 30, verses 10–15.

2 James Shirley, 'Death the Leveller'.

3 *The Brihadaranyaka Upanishad with Commentary of Shankaracharya*, translated by Swami Madhavananda (Advaita Ashrama, 1950), 2.4.

CHAPTER 35 YAMA MEETS RAMANA

1 Sri Ramana Teachings Q&A's, 'Iain McNay and Michael James: What was Ramana Maharshi's death experience?', YouTube. Available online: http://youtube.com/watch?v=DQl_8V4CDS4.

2 The description of the experience in Ramana Maharishi's words is from *The Teachings of Ramana Maharishi*, ed. Arthur Osborne (Rider, 2019), p. 15.

3 Patrick Olivelle, *Upanishads: A New Translation* (Oxford University Press, 2008), Chapter 1.3.10–12.

4 *The Garuda Purana (Saroddhara)*, translated by Ernest Wood and S.V. Subrahmanyam (Panini Office Bhuvaneswari Ashrama, 1911), Chapter 1, verses 26–28.

CHAPTER 36 RAMANA EXPERIENCES YAMA

1 There are five temples, each corresponding to one of the elements: earth, water, fire, air and space. Tiruvannamalai is the fire lingam. The earliest records of this place go back to about 500 CE, at which point it was already famous.

2 Richard Clarke, 'Turtle Rock, Place of Ramana Maharshi's "Second Death Experience"', *Living in the Embrace of Arunchala*, 30 June 2009. Available online: https://richardarunachala.wordpress.com/2009/06/30/turtle-rock-place-of-ramana-maharshis-second-death-experience/ (accessed 23 July 2025).

3 David Goodman, 'An Introduction to Sri Ramana's Life and Teachings', David Godman. Available online: https://www.davidgodman.org/an-introduction-to-sri-ramanas-life-and-teachings/2/.

4 Osborne, *Teachings*, pp. 108–09.

5 *Brahma satyam jagat mithya*.

6 *The Bhagavad Gita, with text and translation by Sri Aurobindo* (Sri Aurobindo Divine Life Trust, 2018), Chapter 2.11–13, pp. 28–29.

7 The famous composition of Sankara's is in thirty-three verses. The story is that Sankara was on his way to Kasi when he saw an old man memorising some rules of grammar. He bursts out with this composition admonishing the man, saying that at the time of death grammar would not save him and he should worship Govinda for release.

Bibliography

BOOKS

Arnold, Edwin. *The Secret of Death*. Little Brown and Company, 1908.

Aryamuni ji, Pandit, Pandit Shivashankar ji and Pandit Harish Chandra ji Vidyalankar. *Rig Veda: Mandala 9*. Sarvadeshik Arya Pratinidhi Sabha, 2010.

Aurobindo, Sri. *The Bhagavad Gita*. Sri Aurobindo Divine Life Trust, 2018.

Aurobindo, Sri. *The Secret of the Veda*. Sri Aurobindo Ashram, 2018.

Badrinath, Chaturvedi. *The Women of the Mahabharata*. Orient Longman, 2008.

Bhattacharji, Sukumari. *The Indian Theogony: A Comparative Study of Indian Mythology from the Vedas to the Puranas*. Cambridge University Press, 1970.

Brahma Purana, Parts 1–4. Motilal Banarasidass, 1955.

Brihadaranyaka Upanishad with Commentary of Shankaracharya, The. Translated by Swami Madhavananda. Advaita Ashrama, 1950.

Brunton, Paul, and Mungala Venkataramaiah. *Conscious Immortality*. Sri Ramanasramam, 2024.

Chinmayananda, Swami. *Discourses on Kathopanishad*. Chinmaya Publications Trust, 1963.

Dayanand Saraswati. *Rig Veda: Mandalas 1–6*. Sarvadeshik Arya Pratinidhi Sabha, 1974.

Debroy, Bibek. *Sacred Songs: The Mahabharata's Many Gitas*. Rupa Publications, 2023.

Deshpande, N.A. (Trans.). *Padmapurana*. Motilal Banarasidass Publishers, 1990.

Dharmadhikari, T.N. *The Maitryani Samhita: Its Ritual and Language*. Adarsh Sanskrit Shodh Sansthan, 2008.

Dutt, Manmatha Nath. *Markandeya Purana*. H.C. Das, Elysium Press, 1896.

Dutt, Manmatha Nath (Trans.). *Mahabharata*, Volumes 1–9. Parimal Publications, 2001.

Dutt, Manmatha Nath (Trans.). *Rig Veda Samhita*. Parimal Publications, 1986.

Eden, Pargiter F. (Trans.). *Markandeya Purana*. Baptist Mission Press, 1904.

Eden, Pargiter F. (Trans.). *Markandeya Purana*. Edited by K.L. Joshi. Parimal Publications, 2004.

Eggeling, Julius (Trans.). *Shatapata Brahmana*, Books 1 and 2. Clarendon Press, 1882.

Gambhirananda, Swami (Trans.). *Eight Upanishads with the Commentary of Sankracharya*, Volume 1. Advaita Ashrama, 2002.

Gandhi, Ramchandra. *The Seven Sages: Selected Essays by Ramchandra Gandhi*. Edited by A. Raghuramaraju. Penguin Books, 2016.

Ganguli, Kisari Mohan, and Pratap Chandra Roy. *The Mahabharata of Krishna Dwaipayana Vyasa*, Volumes 1–3. Oriental Publishing Co., 1842–1895.

Gautam, Chandra Prasanna. *Translation of the Rig Veda Samhita*, Volumes 1–4. Bharatiya Vidya Bhavan, 2014.

Griffith, Ralph T.H. (Trans.). *The Hymns of the Rig Veda*. Edited by Prof. J.L. Shastri. Motilal Banarsidass, 2004.

Griffith, Ralph T.H. *The Rig Veda*. Kindle edition. Evinity Publishing Inc., 2009.

Gupta, Anand Swarup (Ed.). *Vamana Purana*. Varanasi: All India Kashiraj Trust, 1968.

Joshi, Kireet. *Glimpses of Vedic Literature*. Standard Publishers, 2012.

Kashyap, R.L., and Prof. S. Sadagopan. *Rig Veda Samhita*. Sri Aurobindo Kapali Shastri Institute of Vedic Culture, 2005.

Khandelwal, S.N. *Brihaddharma Puranam*. Chowkhamba Sanskrit Series Office, 2014.

Kubler-Ross, Elizabeth. *On Death and Dying*. Scribner, 2016.

Mahadevan, T.M.P. *Sankaracharya*. National Book Trust, 1968.

Mani, Vettam (Ed.). *Puranic Encyclopedia*. Motilal Banarasidass, 1979.

Medhananda, Swami. *Vedantic Cosmopolitanism*. Oxford University Press, 2022.

Mehta, Rohit. *The Dialogue with Death*. Sri Aurobindo Ashram Book Agency, 1972.

Natarajan, A.R. *The Teachings of Ramana Maharishi: An Anthology*. Affiliated East-West Press Ltd, 1995.

Olivelle, Patrick. *Upanishads: A New Translation*. Oxford University Press, 2008.

Osborne, Arthur (Ed.). *The Teachings of Ramana Maharishi*. Rider, 2019.

Prabhupada, Bhakti Vedanta. *Srimad Bhagvatam*, Part 1. Bhakti Vedanta Book Trust, 1975.

Ramana Maharishi, Sri. *The Collected Works of Sri Ramana Maharishi*. Sri Ramanasramam, 1979.

Satvalekar, Shripad Damodar Bhatt. *Mahabharata: Ashvamedhika Parva by Vyasa with Commentary*. Bharat Mudranalay, 1912.

Satvalekar, Shripad Damodar Bhatt. *Maitryani Samhita*. Government Press, 1941.

Shah, Priyabala. *Sri Vishnudharmottara*. New Order Book Co., 1990.

Sharma, Acharya Ram. *Rig Veda Samhita*. Yug Nirman Yojana, 2005.

Sharma, Ganga Sahay. *Rig Veda*. Sanskrit Sahitya Prakashan, 2013.

Sharman, Vishnu. *Panchatantra*. Motilal Banarasidass, 1990.

Shastri, Chinnaswami, and Pattabhirama Shastri, *Tandya Maha Brahmana*. Chowkhamba Sanskrit Sansthan, 1987.

Shastri, J.L. *Linga Purana*. Motilal Banarasidass, 1993.

Shastri, J.L. *Siva Purana*. Motilal Banarasidass, 2002.

Sri Vishnu Purana. Gita Press, 1990.

Srinivasan, K.S. *Ramayana: As Told by Valmiki and Kamban*. Abhinav Publications, 1994.

Sukthankar, S. Vishnu. *The Mahabharata*, 19 volumes. Bhandarkar Oriental Research Institute, 1927–1966.

Tagare, G.V. *Bhagvata Purana*. Motilal Banarasidass, 1999.

Tagare, G.V. *Brahmanda Purana*. Motilal Banarasidass, 2002.

Tulsi Ram (Trans.). *Atharva Veda*. Vijaykumar Govindram Hasanand, 2013.

Valmiki Ramayanam: Uttarakhanda, 13th reprint. Gita Press, 2019.

Vidyalankar, Pandit Harish Chandra ji, and Acharya Baidyanath Shastri ji. *Rig Veda: Mandala 10*. Sarvadeshik Arya Pratinidhi Sabha, 2010.

Vivekananda, Swami. *Reflections*. Om Books International, 2017.

Williams, Monier. A Sanskrit-English Dictionary. Motilal Banarasidass, 1963.

Wilson, H.H. (Trans.). *The Vishnu Purana: A System of Hindu Mythology and Tradition*, Volume 3. Trubner and Co, 1866.

Wilson, H.H. *Rig Veda Sanhita*. The Bangalore Printing and Publishing Co. Ltd, 1946.

Wolfe, Robert. *Ramana Maharishi: Teachings of Self-Realization*. Karina Library Press, 2016.

Wood, Ernest, and S.V. Subrahmanyam (Trans.). *The Garuda Purana (Saroddhara)*. Panini Office, Bhuvaneswari Ashrama, 1911.

JOURNAL ARTICLES

Aurobindo, Sri. 'Agni: The Divine Will Force'. *CWSA* 15: 388–389. Available online: https://incarnateword.in/cwsa/15/agni-the-divine-will-force#p5 (accessed 15 September 2024).

Kapp, Dieter B. 'The Concept of Yama in the Religion of a South Indian Tribe'. *Journal of the American Oriental Society* 102, no. 3 (July–October 1982): 517–521.

Kazanas, Nicholas. 'Archaic Greece and the Veda'. *Annals of BORI* 82, no. 1/4 (2001): 1–42. Available online: http://www.jstor.org/stable/41694629 (accessed 15 September 2024).

Muir, J. 'Yama and the Doctrine of a Future Life, According to the Rig-, Yajur-, and Atharva-Vedas'. *Journal of the Royal Asiatic Society of Great Britain and Ireland* 1, no. 1/2

(1865): 287–315. Available online: http://www.jstor.org/stable/25207657 (accessed 15 September 2024).

Pradhan, Shruti S. 'The Yama-Yamī Sūkta: New Perspectives'. *Annals of BORI* 71, no. 1/4 (1990): 109–38. Available online: http://www.jstor.org/stable/41693520 (accessed 15 September 2024).

Sandness, Adéla. 'Yáma and Sárasvatī: On Perceptions of Death and the Continuity of Life in Early Vedic Literature'. *Annals of BORI* 88 (2007): 81–97. Available online: http://www.jstor.org/stable/41692086 (accessed 15 September 2024).

ONLINE RESOURCES

Sarvapriyananda, Swami. *Katha Upanishad*. Accessed 15 September 2024, https://www.youtube.com/watch?v=MmoxzLIzAas.

'Garuda Purana: Journey to the World of Yama'. Manblunder, 2011. Accessed 15 September 2024, https://manblunder.com/articlesview/garuda-purana-journey-to-the-world-of-yama.

'DeviMaitri(Maitrayani) Upanishad'. Sanskrit Documents, 2013. Accessed 15 September 2024, http://sanskritdocuments.org/doc_upanishhat/maitri.pdf.

'Iain McNay and Michael James: What Was Ramana Maharshi's Death Experience?' YouTube, 2023. Accessed 15 September 2024, https://www.youtube.com/watch?v=DQl_8V4CDS4.

Godman, David. 'An Introduction to Sri Ramana's Life and Teachings'. Accessed 15 September 2024, http://davidgodman.org/an-introduction-to-sri-ramanas-life-and-teachings/.

Aurobindo, Sri. 'Aham Sphurna: Scintillations of Jnana from Ramana Maharishi'. Accessed 15 September 2024, https://tomdas.com/wp-content/uploads/2024/04/aham-sphurana-scintillations-of-jnana-from-ramana-maharshi.pdf.

About the Author

Sudhamahi Regunathan, an author and translator, is former vice chancellor of the Jain Vishva Bharati University. Her books include *Rishabhayan: The Story of the First King* and *Taken Away: The Ordinary Life of a Lama* (co-written with Lama Doboom Tulku, Bloomsbury India, 2024).